LESSONS 4 A TEACHER
HOPE AND ENCOURAGEMENT 4 YOU

Lessons 4 a Teacher

Hope and Encouragement 4 You

To Darren
May these
lessons of faith
encourage you. We
have hope because
we have God.

Stay encouraged,

Sharon Gavin Levy

SHARON GAVIN LEVY

Scripture quotations marked (AMP) are taken from the Amplified Bible, Copyright © 2015 by The Lockman Foundation. Used by permission.

Scripture quotations marked (CEV) are from the Contemporary English Version Copyright © 1991, 1992, 1995 by American Bible Society. Used by Permission.

Scripture quotations marked KJV are from the King James Version of the Holy Bible.

Scripture quotations marked MSG are taken from *THE MESSAGE*, copyright © 1993, 2002, 2018 by Eugene H. Peterson. Used by permission of NavPress. All rights reserved. Represented by Tyndale House Publishers, Inc.

Scripture quoted by permission. Quotations designated (NET) are from the NET Bible® copyright ©1996, 2019 by Biblical Studies Press, L.L.C. http://netbible.com. All rights reserved.

Scriptures taken from the Holy Bible, New International Version®, NIV®. Copyright © 1973, 1978, 1984, 2011 by Biblica, Inc.™ Used by permission of Zondervan. All rights reserved worldwide. www.zondervan.com The "NIV" and "New International Version" are trademarks registered in the United States Patent and Trademark Office by Biblica, Inc.™

Scripture taken from the New King James Version®. Copyright © 1982 by Thomas Nelson. Used by permission. All rights reserved.

Scripture quotations marked NLT are taken from the *Holy Bible*, New Living Translation, copyright © 1996, 2004, 2015 by Tyndale House Foundation. Used by permission of Tyndale House Publishers, Inc., Carol Stream, Illinois 60188. All rights reserved.

ISBN: *978-1-916964-75-4*

To my husband, Harold, for your love, encouragement, and confidence. You're my love and the best kind of best friend.

To my daughter, Nicole Bethany, my heart, my best work and my answer to prayer. Your beautiful heart and moxie are everything.

To my grandchildren, Elan and Maddie, my joys, my heart explosions and my gifts of unimaginable love. You are indeed Grand.

Contents

CHAPTER ONE

Yes! You're A Teacher

Today we're bombarded with so many roles and responsibilities. Some of them we seek, but many we don't. We're mothers, fathers, sisters, brothers, married, single parents, and guardians. We're barbers and bosses, counselors and coaches, lawyers and landscapers and pastors and preachers. You try your best, give your best and do your best at work and when you serve and volunteer in community, church and corporate settings. You build, safeguard and secure your reputation because integrity is important to you. But in addition to all that you are and all that you do, I promise you this: you are also a teacher. You may object and say, "I'm not a teacher. I don't want to teach and don't know how to teach, so I'm far from a teacher." But the fact remains, there's a teacher in everyone, including you!

Although teaching is my profession, each one of us teaches daily. We teach through how we live. It's really that simple. Your students are your children, family members, friends, acquaintances, neighbors, colleagues, church family and even your enemies. You teach your students every day, like it or not. The Scriptures confirm this in 2 Corinthians 3:2 when Paul reminds us that we are living epistles to be seen and read of all men. So, you are indeed an open book unfolding steadily before your worldwide classroom.

Although your students may rarely read an entire book, they read every single word of you. They read your conduct, your countenance, your words, your ways, your attitude, your actions, your dos and your don'ts. Everything about you teaches. Students read you, they study you, they examine you, they assess you, they notate you, they memorize you, they analyze you, they scrutinize you and they test you. Whether desired or not, you are a bona fide teacher and others learn from you every day.

The challenge we face as teachers is that school never ends. There's no dismissal time, no recess, no lunch break, no study halls, no teachers' lounge, no snow days, no holidays, and no summer vacation. Day in and day out, we're front and center in life's classroom with student eyes always on us simply because we're the teacher.

It can be overwhelming, especially when you didn't sign on for a classroom teaching assignment. However, you were recruited to the teaching profession the moment you confessed faith in Christ. The moment you received Him as your Savior, your role and responsibilities expanded and now all eyes are on you. You're no longer only a manager, analyst, entrepreneur, engineer, artist, mechanic or medical tech. Your faith confession forever enlarged your life profession.

When you became a believer, you became a disciple, a follower of Christ and a student of His Word. We're called to read the word, hear the word, study the word, learn the word and do the word. But our call goes beyond being just a student. We're students who are appointed student-teachers. We're being trained, guided, directed and counseled for the purpose of teaching others. As Christians, that's the essence of our assignment—to be trained, guided, directed and counseled by the Word of God and the Holy Spirit so our life pleases God and teaches others. In other words, we do what Jesus did; we follow His example and teach.

Prior to beginning His three-year ministry, Jesus worked as a carpenter and by all accounts, He excelled in this profession. His earthly father, Joseph, trained him, supervised him and celebrated Jesus' carpentry skillsand work ethic. No doubt, Joseph enjoyed a successful carpentry business that blessed his family and the Nazareth community thanks to his eldest son, Jesus. We're told in Luke 2:51-52 that Jesus obeyed Joseph and Mary, submitting Himself to their leadership and supervision. The scripture goes on to say that as Jesus grew and matured, He gained "favor with God and man." Therefore, we know Jesus, the carpenter by profession, was not only a model citizen but a consummate professional who pleased God, Joseph, his supervisor, and His customers, the people of Nazareth.

Yet in spite of His personal and professional success as a carpenter, Jesus had to fulfill the role for which He came, the assignment of teacher or *didaskalos* in Greek. I use the Greek word for teacher because it has special significance to you and me as teachers. According to *Strong's Concordance*, a teacher is one who teaches about the things of God and man's responsibilities to God. Upon beginning his ministry at age thirty, Jesus, the former carpenter and now teacher, taught of God and the way of salvation, showing men the path to a right relationship with God. But more importantly to us, the word *didaskalos* suggests that a person must be "fit" to teach, not only having the knowledge and information to teach but having the character and integrity to teach.

Now we all know Jesus was "fit" to teach, for He pleased God in every area of His life. But the question for you and me is this: Are we "fit" to teach? We can be because God would not call us to teach without equipping us to teach. Therefore, the word *didaskalos* also implies a teacher is one who understands the "work of teaching with the special assistance of the Holy Spirit." And that's what we must rely on in our role as a teacher—the training, guidance, direction and counsel of the Holy Spirit. If people are going to be reading my life, studying my life, examining my life, and learning from my life, I need the Holy Spirit to make me "fit" for my teaching job; I desire the character and integrity needed for this assignment. Don't you?

So yes, you're a teacher. Whether you chose the profession of teaching, were called to it, sent to it or packed up and went to it, remember the life you live before others each day teaches much. That makes you a teacher because Jesus made you a teacher! We must successfully fulfill the role He assigned to all believers in Matthew 28:20—to become His disciples and to teach and make more disciples. We become disciples to teach and make more disciples, to teach and add, and to teach and multiply. And the reality is most of our teaching does not take place in Sunday school, Bible study or any theological classroom. You are teaching most lessons in your home, on the job, in your neighborhood, in your vehicles, in the parking lot, at the mall, at church meetings, at choir practice, in the fitness center, at social events, at the ballpark, on the cell phone, and at the computer. You teach anywhere and everywhere. Be mindful and careful because someone is watching you and learning from you. That's why teachers never get a break; we're always teaching! Thus, the critical thinking questions for you and me must be, "What are students learning from me?" "How can my life become more fit for teaching?" "How can my life teach lessons that please God and help others?"

If these questions perplex you, trouble you, challenge you or pique your interest, *Lesson 4 A Teacher* awaits you.

Lesson 4 A Teacher is my first labor of love for that teacher in you. We're teachers together and all teachers need some on-the-job training and professional development. Fortunately, God provided an incredible 66-book training manual that will make better teachers of us all. In addition, the Holy Spirit, the Master Teacher, will teach us and guide us so that we may teach others. Teachers share ideas, exchange syllabi and lesson plans; teachers work together. Teachers also support each other and learn from each other to perfect their teaching.

I share *Lesson 4 A Teacher: Hope and Encouragement 4 You,* with each of you to perfect your teaching. I share my personal experiences and powerful lessons of trusting God's promises, waiting on God, obeying God, worshipping God, and seeing God in all of life's seasons. There are other lessons as well, lessons with valuable, life-giving scriptures. These are lessons we all must learn, lessons we must live, and lessons we must teach. I share my lessons because that's what teachers do. I share my lessons to give you hope and encouragement because, yes, you're a teacher. You're a teacher with students watching you, students whose lives you can transform.

CHAPTER TWO

Faith Under Fire: When Our Faith is Tested

A few years ago, some women in my church shared devotions on faith as a part of our early morning prayer calls. Their faith messages encouraged and inspired me each week, pointing out the importance of faith in our life. When I was invited to prepare a devotional message, my first thought was on challenges to our faith because I sometimes struggle with my faith during difficult times. So, I questioned, "What happens when our faith is tested and when our faith comes under fire? Is it unusual or can it be expected?" I think we can expect challenges because faith is central to our belief system. We hear messages on faith, we study the word to learn about faith, we pray and ask God to increase our faith, we speak faith, we step out on faith and we even sing about faith. Yet with all of this faith action, I promise you—Your Faith will come under fire; Your Faith will be tested. Nobody's faith is tamper-free; testing and trials will come.

I often hear James the Apostle's advice echo in my heart and mind, "My brethren, count it all joy when you fall into various trials, knowing that the testing of your faith produces patience" (James 1:2-3 KJV). James reminds us that our faith will be tried, tested, and proved so that we can see if our faith is all it's cracked up to be. The testing of our faith develops us, builds our character and makes us mature. While it's painful and distressing, our faith under fire actually benefits us. I recall three examples in the Bible that demonstrate how having our faith under fire is indeed a blessing. Through these examples, we learn this vital lesson: The testing of our faith reveals God's presence, God's plan and God's power.

Sometimes our faith comes under fire through no fault of our own. We're serving God, obeying God, believing God and trusting God. Then out of nowhere, come attacks against us, attacks in our circumstances and situations, attacks from people, spiritual attacks and attacks from this fallen world. In these moments, we're quick to declare, "No weapon that is formed against thee shall prosper; and every tongue that shall rise against thee in judgment thou shalt condemn. This is the heritage of the servants of the LORD, and their righteousness is of me, saith the LORD" (Isaiah 54:17 KJV).

Such is the attack against Shadrach, Meshach, and Abed-Nego, three young Hebrews who served God and held fast to their faith when it came under fire, literally came under fire. Their familiar story, found in Daniel 3:1-30, is about King Nebuchadnezzar, an order to worship an image of gold, their refusal to bow down and the test of the fiery furnace. But the blessing in this test was that the fire had no power over them, their hair was not burned, their clothing not destroyed, and the aroma of smoke was nowhere near them. Why? Because they were not alone in the fire. The Bible said when King Nebuchadnezzar gazed into the hotter-than-hot fiery furnace, he saw a fourth man walking in the midst of Shadrach, Meshach, and Abed-Nego. A King far greater than Nebuchadnezzar was present in the fire with them, protecting them from the flame, heat and smoke. Yes, God could have shut down the furnace, He could have spoken from heaven, He could have sent an earthquake or He could have dispatched angels. God had more options than we had ideas. But rather than do any of those things, God chose to be present with them when their faith came under fire.

And God's presence is with you when your faith is under fire. Sometimes the testing and trials we face seem so overwhelming and we question whether we're going to get through this thing. We also worry that if we do get through, we'll end up bent over, battered, bitter, and scarred, but we must not underestimate the power of God's presence. Just having Him in our life, in the center of every situation, in the fire and flood, in the darkest night and in the lonely, isolated places--just having Him present—makes all the difference. "When thou passest through the waters, I will be with thee; and through the rivers, they shall not overflow thee: when thou walkest through the fire, thou shalt not be burned; neither shall the flame kindle upon thee" (Isaiah 43:2 KJV). What reassurance we have when the fire falls!

Another example of faith under fire comes from the life of Abraham and Sarah, a test of waiting for the son of promise for twenty-five years. Like Abraham and Sarah, our faith is tested when we have to wait a long time for God's promise, when we have to wait on the answer to prayer, and when we have to wait on the desire of our heart. Waiting is painful and we often get discouraged and depressed, but waiting reminds us that God is sovereign, God is in control, and God has a plan. Indeed, God's plan is so much greater than your plan. God's plan is a detailed plan; it includes who, what, where and when. That means you must trust God for His who, what, where and especially His when. "The Lord is not slow in keeping his promise, as some understand slowness. Instead, he is patient with you, not wanting anyone to perish, but everyone to come to repentance" (2 Peter 3:9 NIV). As in the case of Abraham and Sarah, God really does know what he's doing when He allows us to wait and requires us to wait. He knows we're hurting, but He also knows when the time is right. Throughout the Bible, we see phrases like "fullness of time," "according to the time," "process of time," and "in due season." We have to throw away our electronic devices, appointment books and calendars and trust God's "in due season." He alone determines the time the answers will come, and they will definitely come. Always remember, "Hope deferred makes the heart sick, but *when* the desire comes, *it is* a tree of life" (Proverbs 13:12 NKJV). So we must rest in God's sovereignty, rely on His timepiece and trust His plan.

Finally, consider Gideon in Judges 6, who led an Army of 300 against the Midianite Army of over 100,000. How was his faith under fire? God said He was going to use Gideon to deliver Israel out of the hands of the Midianites. But Gideon's faith was tested when he didn't trust the power of God's word. Gideon concluded that his poverty and personal background disqualified him from this monumental assignment. Overwhelmed with fear and insecurity, Gideon lacked confidence. Why would God use him? Sound familiar? Like you and me, Gideon kept seeking reassurance from God by using the wool fleece. I can hear Gideon now. "Father God, I know you'll use me to deliver Your people if the wool fleece is wet and the threshing floor is dry. Okay, Lord. I want to be absolutely certain you're speaking; make the wool fleece dry and the floor wet." Both times God showed His power to do the supernatural and it was Gideon's time to be the mighty warrior of faith God created. When Gideon's 300 blew the trumpets, they watched 100,000 disoriented Midianites run and destroy each other. Gideon knew he didn't defeat the Midianites; the supernatural power of God won that battle.

So when your faith comes under fire because of your own feelings of doubt, fear, unbelief, insecurity and inadequacy, remember God's power brings the victory. It's not about us. It's not about your capacity or your ability, but it's the victorious power of God. "Now thanks *be* to God who always leads us in triumph in Christ" (2 Corinthians 2:14 KJV). Just as God led Gideon to victory with a small limited army, He'll also lead you and me with His unlimited power. "Now unto him that is able to do exceeding abundantly above all that we ask or think, according to the power that worketh in us" (Ephesians 3:20 KJV).

Yes. Expect your faith under fire; know our faith will be tested. When the fiery trials come, be mindful of God's presence to protect you from the flames, heat and smoke. He's with you, a very present help in trouble, promising to never leave you or forsake you. Even if you feel forsaken because of waiting, waiting and more waiting, you're not. Time may be testing your faith in God, but God has a plan. The one who stepped out of time, who created time, and who controls time has a timely plan for you. He is perfect in all of His ways, so trust His timing and trust His plan. Trust Him when you doubt and fear. Trust Him with the guilt and shame. Trust His power always. He's greater than all your sins, all your weaknesses and all your inadequacies. God is what you're not. He's able; He's mighty and He's powerful. When your faith is under fire and when your faith is tested. Rely on Him. God's presence, God's plan and God's power will deliver you, sustain you and embolden you.

CHAPTER THREE

He's Worth the Wait

"But they that wait upon the LORD shall renew their strength; they shall mount up with wings as eagles; they shall run, and not be weary; and they shall walk, and not faint."

(Isaiah 40:31)

I can remember years ago, the choir singing a song from Isaiah 40:31, "They that wait on the Lord shall renew their strength. They shall mount up on wings as an eagle. They shall run and not be weary. They shall walk and not faint." And then the chorus followed with the words "Wait on the Lord," repeated several times, before ending with the command, "Wait, I say, on the Lord!"

What touched my heart in that song was its promise—the promise of being renewed, the promise of ascending high, the promise of running without exhaustion, walking without tiring, and doing it all with supernatural strength. Can you imagine that? I really needed such a promise in my life. So, most of the time, I cried throughout the song because it encouraged me to wait, to walk, to hold on and to trust God. But the tears also flowed because deep down inside, I wondered if God was actually going to come through for me. I was so tired of waiting and I did not want orders to continue to wait on the Lord. I wanted what I wanted and I wanted it now! Yet, in spite of my resistance to waiting, the song's encouraging words assured me of God's promise and His power. Somehow this song offered me a hope that I knew could only come from God. It was a hope based on two things—being willing to wait and knowing who I was waiting on. So, I grabbed that hope and resolved to wait on God to hear and answer my constant prayers.

But waiting is no easy thing. And with my waiting came many unanswered questions. Why do we have to wait? Who really wants to wait? Do some people find waiting easier than others? Is it actually possible to put all your hope in God? Why are some able to wait eagerly for Him? Although I couldn't answer all of these questions, some things became a bit clearer to me. The words "But they that wait upon the Lord" reminded me that people respond differently to waiting when they need something from God. When folks need God to move in their life, not everyone will wait. Some choose to ignore God as well as His power; they rely solely on their own ability, trying to do it all their way and in their own strength. Others start out relying on God but tire when God's timing doesn't work for them. He just takes way too long, so they give up. There are those, however, who choose to Wait, and not just wait for the sake of waiting; they are intentional about it. They wait On the Lord and wait For the Lord. These are the folks who will actually receive and experience the promise of Isaiah 40: "They SHALL renew, they SHALL mount up, they SHALL run and they SHALL walk!" Why? Because they decided to wait and focus their wait on God. They looked in the right direction as they waited!

That's why this song always encouraged me to look to the Lord and keep moving forward even though prayers went unanswered and promises went unfulfilled. Waiting on God meant I had to accept His schedule and His time frame. I didn't like the delay and saw no purpose in it, but I still had to mark time, day after day after day after day. Eventually, I began to see waiting a bit differently. I wasn't just waiting helplessly or hopelessly because I had no alternative; I was waiting on the LORD. In time, I asked myself... Am I going to place my full hope, trust and confidence in God? Can I surrender my life, my plans and my schedule to Him? Do I have the faith to do it? Again, I didn't have the answers, but it seemed God did. So, I tried God's way and God's wait. Even with my little faith and tiny baby steps, my waiting on the Lord shifted. The LORD became my focus, not the things I was praying and waiting for.

That's when it finally hit me! I wasn't waiting on just anybody or some random god; I was waiting on the God of all creation, the Almighty God who made heaven and earth, the One who created me. And since He created me, He certainly understood my impatience, frustration, anxiety and restlessness; God knew I was tired of waiting and crying and crying and waiting. Yes. He knew it. But even so, He still had me waiting... waiting... waiting.

Looking back, I see this "waiting on the Lord" was a powerful process because 'the wait' changed me. And that was an important lesson for me, a crucial lesson for everyone. There is growth "in waiting." While you wait, God produces something in you. Why does He do this?

Because you need it; He's doing what's needed—the necessary thing. *So, while you wait, God works. And while God works, you wait.* He renews you and increases your strength, He empowers you to mount up and soar over life's situations, and He energizes you to run and complete life's marathons. Ultimately, as you wait on God, He fortifies you to walk through life's seasons without **Braking or Breaking**.

It's God's "waiting process"—the hoping, the expecting, the anticipating, the looking-eagerly-to-God process—that delivers three essential life lessons: Don't give up, Don't give out, and Don't give in. How difficult it is to hear these directives when time beats you down in the midst of waiting. We hear: "Hold on... Don't give up... Don't give out... Don't give in." And the reality is we don't even know what those words mean, especially in uncertain times—Don't give up? Don't give out? And Don't give in? We don't want words; we want a way out! But the waiting-on-the-Lord process endeavors to shift our view from looking for a way out to looking for a way through. The bottom line is this—as we wait, *God doesn't want us to flee; He wants us to flourish.*

This may be a tough lesson, but it's a life-changing lesson. In our journey through life, one thing is certain: We will experience times when we have to wait on the Lord; there's no other option, nothing else we can do. There are times when our troubles drag on and on, times when loved ones continually crush our hearts, times when struggles outweigh our strength, times when problems seem greater than solutions, and times when questions far outnumber answers. That's when all we can do is wait, wait on God without giving up.

So, when we're encouraged to hold on and hang in there, the wisdom words "Don't give up" translate to "Don't give up on God; He won't let you down, He won't leave you alone and He won't abandon you no matter what." "Don't give up" means: You think you won't make it, but you will; you think you can't do it, but you can. You think you don't have it, but you do. Since God's got you, you got this. Don't give up on His Word; it's prevailed for thousands of years and carried generations safely and satisfactorily through life; it can and will carry you too. Trust His word and don't give up on God's promises.

That's why the Isaiah 40:31 scripture and song mean so much to me. I've waited in the past, I'm waiting today and I'm pretty certain there's some "waiting on God" in my future. But the real secret to waiting is to focus on the Who and not the What of our wait. Too often, we're concerned about what we are waiting for. It could be the right job, the right mate, the right ministry, the right status, the right medical report, the right home, the right behavior, or the right situation. Setting our sights on the circumstances alone is guaranteed to frustrate and decrease our faith as we wait. Because all we do is constantly turn our attention to what we don't have, what is wrong, what has not happened and what is lacking in our lives. We fight this ongoing battle between today's despair and tomorrow's desires. And like the psalmist, we'll find ourselves moaning, "Why art thou cast down, O my soul? And why art though disquieted in me?" (Psalm 42:5) But the answer is simple. We're cast down, we're distressed and we're discouraged because we're looking for the special delivery instead of looking to the Special Deliverer.

But when we look to God, hope in Him and trust His Word, relief comes, strength surges and our heart sings, "I feel like going on." God's word is full of promises that shout at us, "Don't give up!" There are scriptures that pertain to every problem, every crisis, and every situation we face. You must look for the promises that relate to your dreams, your situation, your family and your future. Then hold these scriptures tight when faced with a tsunami of doubt. Wait out the storm and don't give up. If we cling to His promises as tightly as we cling to our pain, God will not disappoint. He moves in us so we can handle today's delays and tomorrow's challenges. As we embrace His Word, we mount up, ascend high and wait on Him with patience and expectation, knowing He's not going to let us down. He's greater than all our stuff! All of it! That's why we must wait on God and never give up.

Another lesson the "waiting-on-God" process teaches us is—Don't give out. We may be waiting on God, speaking His Word and holding tight to our faith. And perhaps we've been doing this day after day, week after week and month after month. Maybe even "year after year." But when waiting continues with no results, frustration sets in and we're likely to holler, "Really, God? Do you know how long I've been praying about this? Do you realize it's been a week, a month, a year, a decade? Are you serious, Lord? I can't do this, not another day. Please!" Yes. We often tire and suffer battle fatigue as we wait. But God's "waiting process" is designed to teach us endurance, perseverance and resilience. And we need all three and more as we journey through life. Therefore, we can't give out; we have to keep going. When we're physically exhausted, emotionally weary and our faith walk falters, God's "waiting process" prompts us to continue on the journey. It's necessary to trust God moment by moment, look for answered prayers daily, expect the promise in this season, and wait on God day by day, hour by hour, even minute by minute. There is never a right time to put the brakes on your faith! This is not the hour to give out; no hour is. Though you are tempted, don't stop. It's true that waiting a long time is hard, but holding on just one more second can make all the difference; this second is likely the one that leads to success. That's why we must not give out; we've got to keep moving forward, trusting and hoping in God. He's the Light before us, the Guide beside us and the Protector behind us; He surrounds us. Through waiting, we soon learn that His strength lights the way, pushes us forward and even carries us through life. If we are determined to never give out, God makes sure we never give out. Our pace may slow but we persevere; we walk on, we move forward and we don't give out.

And because God doesn't want us to give out, He certainly doesn't want us to give in. We can't give in to the pressures of life and the difficult circumstances we all face. We can't give in to anxiety and depression when opposition threatens our hopes and dreams. We can't give in to challenges or challenges designed to break our hearts and spirits. We must hold fast to our desires. If we've waited a day or a decade, it counts for something; it's territory we've gained through our faith and waiting on God. To give in would be "a surrender," and we must surrender nothing and give back nothing despite fatigue, discouragement and disappointment. We must never give in, never surrender our hope, no matter how long we wait.

When we finally grasp, "Don't give up, Don't give out, and Don't give in," we understand that waiting on God is not a passive process but a productive one. It's productive because learning to wait, deciding to wait and accepting the wait require strength, a God-renewed strength. When you learn to wait, you resolve to never give up, never give out, and never give in; and God, Himself, renews you. You emerge anew and changed for the better, the Isaiah 40:31 version of you. God produces newness in your life, your faith and your experience. You will Mount up—that is... you will ascend, spring up, rise, go up over and you will extend your boundary and go higher than even you expected!

Finally, you will run. You won't jog, but you will have the capacity to run very swiftly. In other words, you'll be re-energized with the passion, enthusiasm and speed to pursue. And although you have the ability to run, you will have the wisdom to walk because walking suggests you will maintain a lifestyle in which you continue to go on and move forward; you will proceed as one who is no longer weary, no longer dragging or discouraged but one who is ready to move, one who is starting to move and one who will continue to move. That's why we must learn this lesson: Don't give up, Don't give out and Don't give in. Wait on God, He won't forget you and He won't fail you. He's forever the same. Wait on God. Whatever the situation, whatever the temptation and whatever the duration, remember Isaiah 40:31, "They that wait on the Lord." Wait on God. He's worth the wait.

CHAPTER FOUR

Why I Worship

Worship songs ring out in our sanctuaries. "We worship you..." "Lord, I worship You ..." "Come let us worship the Lord..." "Worship Him, Christ, the Lord." "Receive my worship, all of my worship."

I often think about why we worship. Yes, the Bible tells us to "worship the Lord in the beauty of holiness," and the word "worship" appears in the Bible more than one hundred times. That alone says worship is central to our relationship with God. Worship, along with prayer and praise, is unquestionably a major part of our spiritual life. I recall the time when churches placed a tremendous emphasis on revitalizing worship in their Sunday services. Churches of every tradition and denomination abandoned their customary practices, replacing them with "praise and worship" segments that included musicians, singers, and sometimes dancers. In the Black church, "testimony service," once led by deacons and devotional leaders, was replaced by "praise and worship," led by psalmists and worship leaders. Just as Jesus instructed the woman at the well to worship the Father in Spirit and in truth, our spiritual leaders encourage us to worship God sincerely as never before. We're told to "close in," "enter in," and "draw nigh" to worship God. In fact, a whole new genre of music—worship music—has evolved to create and enhance the atmosphere for private and public devotion. Worship, whether our collective gathering or private meeting with God, is a far-reaching spiritual experience in today's church. No matter its form, occasion or tradition, worship has a divine purpose for everyone; for everyone is called to worship.

When we answer God's call to worship, what do we expect from God and what does God expect from us? On our journey from "new worshipper" to "true worshipper," we must move from just seeking the worship experience to seeking the God of the experience. We may crave electrifying spiritual action in our worship, but do we crave the Holy Spirit's compelling action that accompanies our worship? When we worship God, the Holy Spirit is working in us, changing, rearranging, correcting and perfecting, and then drawing us back to worship again and again, for God desires authentic and continual worship. That's why we must guard against being a "worshipper" in name only or a "worshipper" for acclaim only because worship is not a self-directed act to enhance our spiritual image. Instead, we should seek the transformational power of worship and understand this: Yes, worship is indeed about spiritual image; but it's about God's image, not our image. Our worship should honor, extol and reverence Him since true worship is a God-designed and God-centered experience, a personal and private encounter that must and will have profound public results. In other words, true worship produces people whose conduct, character and conversation reflect the image of God. Yes, His image. That's the purpose of worship: God's image!

I think about worship in terms of looking at family photographs. We all have our favorite family photos, pictures of our spouse, our wedding, our parents and grandparents, our siblings and our many friends and loved ones. But the most prized family photographs are those of our children. From the time our children arrive, we take lots of pictures because we want to captureevery precious moment. We marvel at seeing them growand change, especially when they begin to look like us. I remember when our daughter was an infant, everyone said she looked just like her Dad, and I must admit, she did. As she grew into a young woman, however, she began to resemble me. Nothing pleased me more. So can you imagine God's reaction as we look more and more like Him?

But let's remember that children resembling their parents goes beyond the physical features. It includes having their parent's behavior, disposition, movements, attitudes, expressions, speech patterns and voice quality, all characteristics a child acquires after living with a parent day in and day out. This likely explains why adopted children often favor their adoptive parents because the ways of the parents become the ways of the child. And God certainly wants this for His children. He wants us to become more and more like Him, acquiring His ways and disposition, adopting His movements and speech patterns, expressing His attitudes and viewpoints and growing to look like Him. When we worship, this will happen because true worship produces an image change;

it re-shapes and re-creates our image into the image of God.

When we think about God's image, remember that God created only mankind in His own image. God created man in His likeness to walk in His authority, giving man special thought and consideration above and beyond all other creations. While God spoke other creations into being with "let there be" or "let the," God planned mankind's existence with "let us make." And so He did. God formed mankind, male and female, through the work of His own mighty hands and in His own righteous image and likeness, according to Genesis 1:27. Thus, man was picture-perfect and ready for a flawless family portrait with God. We see God in this portrait and mankind looking exactly like Him, clothed in God's disposition, God's movements, God's expressions, God's attitude, God's mannerisms, God's speech patterns and God's righteousness. Mankind looked like God. But then the picture changed.

Their act of disobedience in Genesis 3:6-7 transformed Adam and Eve as well as all mankind forever. Now Adam and Eve did not look like God, destroying their place in the family portrait. Mankind reflected their own image, an imperfect image from disobeying God, an evil, spiteful, crafty, self-centered image, and a sinful image and likeness that would pass to all mankind. No longer would man be created according to Genesis 1:27 in the image of God, but from this point forward, mankind would emerge in Adam's likeness after his image. "When Adam had lived 130 years, he had a son in his own likeness, in his own image; and he named him Seth. after his image" (Genesis 5:3 NIV). What a transformation this was when mankind's image and likeness changed from the image of God to the image of a disobedient, sinful man. We see why it was absolutely necessary to photoshop mankind from God's family portrait.

Yet in spite of mankind's actions, God wasdetermined to restore us to the family photo. God's love was greater than man's disobedience, greater than man'sevil, greater than man's sin and greater than man's distorted image. God's love provided the remedy for us— salvation— through faith in Jesus Christ. With salvation, we become new creations in Christ, born again into God'sfamily with our designated place in the family portrait. But while we're once again positioned in the photograph with God, eternally secured by God's DNA, the reality is we don't look much like Him—at first.

That's where worship comes in. Worship is an image-changing process designed to restore us to our Genesis 1:27 appearance. True worship is that loving encounter we share in the presence of God, Our Father. The more we're in His presence, the more we embrace His ways, His words, His walk and the more we obey Him. With true worship, we look more like God each day. No paternity test is needed because one look at our face, one word from our mouth, one step in our walk, and one act from our heart show who our Daddy is.

Through worship, God informs, transforms and conforms us to the image of His Son, Jesus. In worship, God informs us of who He is. He reveals His love, mercy, grace and power to forgive. When we experience God's patience and compassion, we see areas where we fall short, areas we must submit to Him. And God transforms us even as we surrender those areas to Him. The Holy Spirit does the transforming work, placing the mirror of God's perfection in our faces so that we desire and strive for His image each day. In our striving, the Holy Spirit conforms us to the image of Christ, our elder Brother, fitting us for the family photo. It's a continual act of love because God wants us all in the family photo. It's incomplete without you and me. So, as we worship, understand that it's a process where God works and we win. Since every father wants all of his children to gather from near and far to be in the family photo, let us worship willingly, humbly, gratefully and expectantly, knowing worship is a privilege with power. For in the worship process, God informs us, transforms us and conforms us.

When I suggest true worship is a God-designed and God-centered experience, a personal and private encounter that will have profound public results, I mean this: True worship and being a true worshipper is not an experience that is centered in public display during worship services, spiritual conferences or the mega-gatherings so common today. Such demonstrations of love for God are good and have their place. But true worship is that God-centered experience that comes straight from the word, that experience that causes us to bow down before God so that He rises up within us. We fall down, but He gets up! Worship is that day-in-and-day-out experience with God that has us looking more like Him, thinking more like Him, speaking more like Him, acting more like Him and loving more like Him. If we're worshippers, people will see that we look more and more like our father in the family portrait because worship changes our image to look like God.

Therefore, we must allow worship to produce what God desires—children who look just like Him. Worship blesses God but blesses us more because it transforms us; it restores us to our rightful place in God's family portrait. Through sincere and sustained worship, our image becomes a reflection of the image of God once again; thus, others see more of God and less of us. But if you're worshipping without a change in your likeness and if you're worshipping an experience more than worshipping God, it's time to renew your commitment to worship God's way. He desires this family portrait: God at the center with all of His children gathered around, each one looking like Him. Worship creates this picture, so consider what God is doing in you when you worship. Let God do it and then smile for the camera.

CHAPTER FIVE

God Promised

"I will never leave you nor forsake you." Hebrews 13:5, NKJV

"Let us hold fast the confession of our hope without wavering, for He who promised is faithful."

Hebrews 10:23, NKJV

There's power in a promise, even when a pandemic holds the entire world hostage. I think about the early days of the Covid-19 shutdown. Initially, we thought we'd be confined to our homes for a week or so. A week turned into two, three, four weeks and then there was no talk of an end. But unfortunately, there was much talk of Covid's rapid spread, its increasing hospitalizations, and the many deaths locally and in the nearby New York/New Jersey metropolitan area. It soon became apparent both medical professionals and political leaders did not know the course of the disease or the duration of the shutdown. We were all in unknown territory, awake but living in a dream, alive but facing possible death, and alert yet reeling in a catastrophic movie. It was both surreal and unreal. It was a remake of the classic *The Day the Earth Stood Still*. But my personal remake was the horrific *The Day the Earth and Time and Life Stood Still*.

Did I ever need God in this pandemic moment. Until its arrival, I was content with the historical time in which I was placed—indoor toilets, running water, automobiles, washing machines, air conditioners. I always praised God for His wisdom in not placing me in the 1700s, 1800s or even early 1900s because He knows I'm not an outhouse or horse and buggy person. "But a pandemic, God? Worldwide shutdown? Really"? History classes taught me about the Black Plague and other deadly epidemics, but given technology and modern medical advancements, I never expected to face such peril in my lifetime. It was out of the realm of possibilities or so I thought. The pandemic prompted questions, fear, questions, prayer, questions, fear, questions, prayer. A whole lot of fear and a whole lot of prayer. How was God to get through to me in the crashing thunder of pandemic fear? Where was that "still small voice" that Elijah heard? Would I hear it in the isolation's deafening sound? "God, I need to hear from You. What is going on here? There's a pandemic, everything's shutdown, we can't have church, we can't go to work, people are dying, we're wearing masks, there are food and supply shortages, it's really happening, this is real, there's no vaccine, and they don't know when this will end. What is this? What is happening? What? What"? Pandemic fear took hold.

I don't know exactly when, but I do know that fear scooted over as the "still small voice" whispered, "I will never leave you nor forsake you." I don't know exactly how, but this Hebrews 13:5 scripture, one of my favorite hope-sustaining promises, was hijacked in those early Covid days. Maybe it was hijacked by the swiftness of the shutdown: one day, it was "business as usual," and the next, it was business as unusual. "We're canceling church on Sunday. Move your on-campus class to the online platform, and wear a mask to enter this store." Maybe it was the barrage of texts to pray for Covid patients, Covid hospitalizations, and families with Covid deaths; for those incessant prayer requests bombarded me day and night. Or maybe God's promise was hijacked because life as I knew it was "turned upside down" for me and absolutely everyone. Covid assaulted the global community; no one escaped. It was beyond frightening for a moment. Yes, for a minute or two, fear ran rampant, tightening its grip around me, until God's reminder, "I will never leave you nor forsake you." When the "still small voice" spoke those resounding words, I heard, I listened, and I remembered WHAT God promised and THAT God promised.

God promised that He would never leave me nor forsake me. So, in all of life's difficulties, in all the chaos, in all the troubles and trials, and in the midst of a worldwide pandemic, God is with me and He's with you. He is mindful of me. He thinks about me and He thinks about me thinking about all that worries and troubles me. But God knows these worries are my portion, my assignment to grow me and glow me. Like the blessings He gives, we're given burdens, trials, tests, temptations and yes, even a worldwide pandemic, a pandemic with a purpose.

God sees this pandemic assignment and whether He has sent it or just allows it, the effect on me is the same. It's a challenge that depletes me, saps my strength, thrashes my hope, and bullies my faith. But while it may deplete, it doesn't defeat! Why? Because God's promise is our lifeline—a life-giving, life-sustaining, and life-restoring lifeline. When God promises to never leave me in Hebrews 13:5, He's promising to never loosen His grip on me. God will never stop holding on to me, no matter what I go through. Even when I manufacture my mess, create my own chaos and design my own drama, God will be there holding me tight.

God's promise is sure and His commitment is secure. He won't fail me. He won't fail to uphold me; He won't fail to watch me like an adoring Mother watching her young. God promised to keep me safe and keep my head above water in a flood, a tsunami, and in the tidal waves of life. And though I still can't swim, our loving God will uphold me. He will not let me sink because He promised to never leave me.

God also promised this: He will never forsake me. I may be isolated, alone, and held captive by a microscopic infection, but God will never abandon me. He promised His presence all day, every day, anywhere and everywhere. If I journey to the mountain of victory or the valley of despair, and when I travel life's painful and desolate terrain, God will not abandon me there. He'll be with me always-in the wealthy places, the healthy places, the fiery places and the miry places. If I'm there, He's there with me because He promised. I may wander away from His path or I may reject His path altogether. I may plan my own itinerary, or life's whirlwinds may control the destination. But whatever my path, whatever my location, and no matter the years or the wandering's duration, God will not desert me.

Even on your worst day, you cannot deter or diminish God's promise. My own sin, pride, and rebellious heart may entrap me, yet God is with me. When I'm cornered and captive, languishing and suffering, God still won't turn His back on me. He won't forsake me and leave me behind; He'll never leave me to my own devices, helpless and hopeless. He's teaching me many lessons, especially in a pandemic with a purpose. God will stay with me, and I will survive. He hears me, and He helps me: God is my safe place. He's your safe place too.

So even in the Covid-19 pandemic and in all of life's pandemics, God's promise resonates and reassures me that He's with me. "I will never leave you nor forsake you." You and I face nothing alone. I can now exhale as I hear the "still small voice" continue to say, "We're in this

God Promised

together. We're in that together. We're in everything together." God promised.

CHAPTER SIX

Words Say It Loud

"Let me finish." "You're not hearing me." "Are you okay." "I'm fine." "Why didn't you talk to me?" "What's wrong?" "There you go again." "You don't listen." "You're shutting down." "Why didn't you?" "You should have." "You shouldn't have." "You always." "You never."

How many times have these and other words built a wall of anger, frustration, and blocked communication? All too often for me, such words have produced pain and meant a missed opportunity for minds to understand and hearts to connect. Words really are a serious matter when building bridges, opening gates, and repairing dams.

What we speak, why we speak, when we speak, and how we speak are all critical when we communicate or try to communicate. Our inspiration, our motivation and our expectation make it or break it when we speak. It's such a natural process, those words flowing from my mouth, but too often, it becomes a natural disaster because I fail. I mess up. I do serious damage. How in the world can a Christian do that?

Everyone has so much to say about words and speaking—our communication. I'm amazed by the sermons preached, the books written, the courses taught, the theories advanced and the communication communicated. Words, words, and more words to help us with our words, words, and more words. Yet with all that word-action, we still "don't get it right." Our marriages dissolve, relationships disintegrate, families disconnect, self-esteem disappears and dreams die all because of words.

Words are extremely important to me, not only as a long-time English professor who loves words—reading them, writing them, evaluating them, editing them, grading them and praising them—but as one who loves to speak them and one who is never at a loss for them. I do words. I love words. I believe a word is worth a thousand pictures.

For me, the true value of words is centered in my faith, my conviction that words are power, my belief that no words are greater than God's word, His words that have a purpose, His words that produce, His words that protect, and His words that always keep their promise. (You would think that I'd do better with my words, given my faith. But I'm sincerely working on doing better with my words, given my faith.)

When I think about God's words and how God speaks, I go back to the beginning, where God shows the significance of words to me. In the first chapter of Genesis, His creation came about through His spoken word... "God said," "Let there be," "God called, God said." Those first words spoken were words that created, words that brought life, words that showered light on dark. His word alone transformed the earth, a place without form, a desolate, empty place, an obscure, void and dark place, a watery wasteland where His spirit lingered to speak light. Imagine that, "speaking" light, not "seeing" light. Can this suggest that the purpose of words is to shine a light on what is dark, establish life from barren ruins, and create something useful and good? God spoke to darkness, and He spoke to a void, bringing light to both. Then can our words bring light to a dark situation? Can our words shape and order what's wasted and without value? Can our words bring meaning to chaos and desolation?

Didn't God use His spoken word in Genesis to create the world He desired, the world He deemed "good," the world He owned, the world His creations would inhabit, and the world where His image-bearers would reside and rule? It's not a big leap, then, to conclude that words create our world. Our words create the place where we will dwell. Our words create the climate, the atmosphere, the topography, the terrain, and the surroundings: Our words do all that. They shape our circumstances and situations. So, what are we doing then? More importantly, what are we saying? How are we handling our words? Or are our words handling us? Do we understand the worth of our words? And do we understand the weight of our words? Do you consider the worth and the weight of your words? Do you think about their power, value, significance, and importance? This is quite a challenge for you and me.

I'm reminded of the amusing expression that advises us to "shoot first and ask questions later" when threatened. Unfortunately, we often treat our communication this way. We're too quick to discharge words and way too trigger-happy to shoot others with "a piece of our mind." Our words come out fast, hitting the target and destroying everything in their path. When, in fact, we should first ask questions: "What should I say? How should I say it? When should I say it? Should I say it at all?"

But the reality is our mouth is our assault weapon of choice, so we're forced to deal with its aftermath. It's not a pretty picture, but it's the one our words paint. Careless words damage and destroy, and I dare say I've been both victim and perpetrator. You've been both too. Whether we endure the pain of hurt or the pain of guilt, it's a pain either way, pain inflicted by words. If we could just learn to be more skillful and purposeful with words, recognizing the power our words hold. It's a struggle, a daily struggle, but it's our collective challenge.

Think about the instruction God provides. God's word teaches us how to use our words to build, to create and to repair. God not only teaches the significance of words and the creative ability of words, but He also teaches the worth of words and the weight of words, giving us principles for words that heal rather than harm. We may not always get it right, but we sure need to get it. We need to give communication the time and energy it deserves. We should be thoughtful and intentional, even humble, when we speak. I've listened, I've learned and I've lived some things, but I still must work on my words. I understand speaking as well as listening are key components of communication but my focus here: my words, my words, my words. My words need structure, my words need order, my words need direction, and my words need control; and I find throughout God's word guidance for my words, guidance for my communication and guidance for every conversation.

God knows we need help with what we say, the content of our message. We need Him to order when we speak; His time is on time. Only His wisdom unfolds the mystery of our hearts when we try but fail to speak, converse, connect and understand each other. Even before our out-of-control words launch, His power alone tempers the atmosphere. He's the ultimate thermostat. And whatever we hope our words accomplish, when it's all said and done, God alone can say when it's all said and done.

It's really quite simple when you consider how God wants to filter our communication. Many scriptures showcase the power and potential of our words. These have directed me to observe five critical areas in every conversation and in every attempt to communicate. If we want words that work, we must look inward, examine our words and strive to master all five parts— Communication's Content, Communication's Clock, Communication's Climate, Communication's Context and Communication's Conclusion.

I cringe when I think of Communication's Content— the words that we speak and the message that we share—because I really butchered the scripture about "speaking the truth in love" years back. Like many people, I believed that Ephesians 4:15, "but, speaking the truth in love," gave me license to speak the "truth" as long as I spoke it in "love." That meant I could evaluate situations, critique people, resolve conflicts, direct activities, pose questions and demand answers, all from the vantage point of my standard of "truth" and my degree of "love." But as you can imagine, both truth and love can sometimes be faulty in our lives and they proved to be faulty in mine.

I was working on a group project and having difficulty getting some things completed by other group members. During the course of this project, I attended a meeting in which I took the opportunity to share my view of the ineffectiveness and inefficiency of other group members and their work. They were shocked and outraged by the "truth" I spoke, and their faces were aghast as I proceeded to verbally assess their inadequate performance. But I left the meeting quite pleased that I spoke honestly and clearly communicated my "truth-filled," unsolicited opinion.

The next morning, however, I ran into a major problem during my prayer and meditation time when God clearly communicated His unsolicited opinion of my words and behavior at the meeting the night before. I defended myself with, "I spoke the truth in love. What's wrong?" Opening the Bible to Ephesians 4:15, I re-read the scripture, hoping to justify my behavior at the meeting. "See. There it is. It says, 'but, speaking the truth in love...' That's why I said what I said last night."

Of course, God had a response, "Keep reading." So, I continued reading Ephesians 4 on and on and on until I reached verse 29. "Let no corrupt communication proceed out of your mouth, but that which is good to the use of edifying, that it may minister grace unto the hearers." Two words, "minister grace," suddenly slapped me in the face, forcing me to question myself. "Did your words 'minister grace' yesterday?" I quietly repeated those words, "Minister grace, minister grace, minister grace." Wow! Really? My words have to "minister grace" to those hearing even as I "speak truth in love." What a revelation. That scripture re-directed my heart and my mind about what I speak and the content of my communication. Since then, "Minister Grace" has challenged me to be more careful about the information, the message, and the words I speak to others because communication's content must "minister grace" to people. In other words, our words must "benefit, help, build up, impart grace, be a blessing" to those hearing. Given that tall order, I checked every bible version and translation just to confirm the "minister grace" requirement.

In a moment, I became less arrogant about my "right" and "obligation" to "speak truth" in so-called "love." Because the reality is most of us focus more on "speaking" and less on "loving" in our communication with others. As I continued to think about the "minister grace" part, I began to realize that "minister grace" mirrors God's way of speaking, God's communication style. God ministers grace to us because all of His word edifies and benefits us. We're enriched, instructed, strengthened, and increased by what God says. Are others increased, instructed, enriched and strengthened by what we say? Maybe they are sometimes but probably not often enough.

Our words influence the lives of others. Our words may create or destroy, advance or hinder, elevate or diminish. It's our choice. My demeaning words to my team added nothing. My self-righteous tirade was a temper tantrum my team didn't deserve. I now understand to "minister grace" with our words requires more than casual consideration of what we want to say; it also requires the wisdom and self-control to say nothing at all. God's word sums it up best, "A fool vents all his feelings, But a wise man holds them back" (Proverbs 29:11 NKJV).

I bet a wise man also knows that timing is everything when it comes to our words. The right words at the wrong time are as disastrous as the wrong words at any time. We are definitely on the clock when it comes to our communication, Communication's Clock. I remember when my husband and I were enrolled in Biblical Counseling courses learning key principles about communication. The issue of timing came up in the context of talking with children. Our wise instructors stressed the importance of waiting for the right time to communicate concerns with young people. They further stated that even the most critical conversations must be timed right, many requiring a "cooling-off" period before the first word is spoken.

Wouldn't you know we had to practice this communication lesson when our teenage daughter went to a party without our permission? When I stopped by her room to say, "Good night," I found it empty. Oh, the words that were forming in my mouth! The moment, the emotions, and the impending words are a saga for another time and another book. But fortunately, my husband and I recognized that this was a "timing-is-everything" event. We waited, believe it or not, two days before we talked with our party-goer about mysteriously disappearing from home and magically appearing at the party. Waiting worked wonders. And since waiting helped me that time, I'm now more mindful about timing and ever aware of communication's clock. "Like apples of gold in settings of silver Is a word spoken at the right time" (Proverbs 25:11 AMP).

I've found that speaking at the right time also promotes the right attitude and creates the right tone. Words are often victims of the surroundings, the environment, and the weather where they're placed. We never speak words in isolation. Words arrive amidst context and conditions, and words arrive amidst filters that may soften, sharpen, intensify or obscure their meaning. Words rest on climate, on atmosphere, and on a location where listeners may thrive, survive or die. It all depends on Communication's Climate, the climate we create with our mood and movement, our temperature and tone, our voice and volume, and our demeanor and disposition. We create it. While we have no control over winter, spring, summer or fall, we have total control over communication's climate. We become the all-powerful meteorologists extraordinaire. We not only forecast the weather conditions, but we create, cultivate, and produce them.

It's tough being a meteorologist, especially when we deny climate change and our climate-control responsibility. Indeed, I'm accountable for how I say what I say and the atmosphere I create. While I claim to want a successful conversation, I really just want to drop my words, so you can pick them up and then we both go about our business. But it's not that easy. There's a positive and productive way to do and say everything. We have to find it, search for it, pursue it, grab it and use it. Climate matters to communication like it matters to the earth. The climate can nourish and nurture or it can ravage and ruin. It's your choice. You're in charge of communication's climate. "By patience *and* a calm spirit a ruler may be persuaded, And a soft *and* gentle tongue breaks the bone [of resistance]" (Proverbs 25:15 AMP). Your words can nourish and nurture and your words can ravage and ruin—you choose. Welcome to Meteorology 101.

If you think the climate in communication is a challenge, then understanding the context in communication will absolutely mystify you. "Why is all this necessary," you ask, "when I just want to speak?" You're welcome to speak but understand words have context, Communication's Context. Words are never ever about just this moment, just this meeting, just this incident, just this event, or just this time. Words come with a history, an origin, an ancient past; words existed long before you. I have a history, too, a history that forges my narrative. I have experiences, I have successes and failures, and I have regrets and disappointments; there have been shout-outs and shame, battles and blame, starts and stops, glitches and gains. And words have been a part of it all, pushing me forward or pulling me back. Words and I are deeply entwined, an entanglement sparking laughter or inciting tears. I bring words, my words, to every conversation and to every attempt to communicate. Such is my story, your story, our story, a story controlled by context.

It may be wise to remember the context when you speak. Your spoken words may connect someone to another time and place or another conversation. Your words may resurrect a painful past or a past pain. Your words may ignite a nuclear reaction and unexpected response. And you're left pondering, "What did I say? What did I do? What just happened?" It may be nothing personal; it may have nothing to do with you and everything to do with context. The past collided with the present and set off an explosion that may impact the future. The words you spoke are not new. Every word, phrase, sentence and expression is securely wrapped in context. We then must take care as we approach others when we converse, remembering they bring a singular history and a personal narrative to the encounter.

A singular history and personal narrative—that's what we all have in common and that's what underlies each conversation. Everyone's singular history and personal narrative carefully listen when you open your mouth to speak. They remember the past, words someone whispered, words someone promised, words proclaimed, words shared, words shouted, words someone lied, words someone denied; they remember them all as you speak. You must be mindful of context, remember it and use the knowledge in every conversation, especially the really important ones. Heaven forbid that our words shatter the shattered, disappoint the disappointed or mislead the misled. Holding back, saying less or saying nothing at all is fine. When it comes to context, it's best to follow this wisdom: "He who has knowledge restrains *and* is careful with his words, And a man of understanding *and* wisdom has a cool spirit (self-control, an even temper)" (Proverbs 17:27 AMP).

One thing about communication, conversations, and speaking is knowing when you've said enough, when you've made your point, and when you've fulfilled your purpose. Since I've done my share of speaking, I've seen the good, the bad and the ugly come straight from my mouth. I've learned much, but I've much to learn. Sometimes I've learned the hard way and sometimes I've gotten it right. Now moving forward, I want forward-moving words, words that inspire, that elevate, that uplift, motivate, encourage, guide, protect, comfort, sooth, move, and words that heal and reveal; I want any and all words that move me and you forward. I know it'll require lessons from God's word, inspiring lessons on Communications Content, Clock, Climate, Context and Conclusion. I want to live, demonstrate and walk out lessons about the worth and weight of words like:

CONTENT

"Words from the mouth of the wise are gracious, but fools are consumed by their own lips." Ecclesiastes 10:12 NIV

"Your speech should always be gracious and sprinkled with insight so that you may know how to respond to every person." Colossians 4:6 CEB

"All spoke well of him and were amazed at the gracious words that came from his lips. "Isn't this Joseph's son?" they asked." Luke 4:22 NIV

CLOCK—CLIMATE

"The heart of the righteous thinks carefully about how to answer [in a wise and appropriate and timely way], But the [babbling] mouth of the wicked pours out malevolent things." Proverbs 15:28 AMP

CONTEXT

"Those who guard their mouths and their tongues keep themselves from calamity."

Proverbs 21:23 NIV

"The tongue of the wise uses knowledge rightly, But the mouth of fools pours forth foolishness." Proverbs 15:2 NKJV

I am challenged, convicted, and convinced that my words, timing, attitude, motivation, and purpose in communication require much growth, daily growth, and continued growth. What about you? Have you thought about your words? Your words say it loud. My words say it loud. All words say it loud.

Our words are seeds we plant in the fertile ground of a heart, mind and soul. We must surrender our words and submit our communication and every conversation to God—the words, the timing, the attitude, the motivation, and the purpose—because words say it loud. Like the Psalmist, let this be our plea, "Let the words of my mouth and the meditation of my heart. Be acceptable in Your sight, O LORD my strength and my Redeemer" (Psalm 19:14 NKJV).

CHAPTER SEVEN

Keep Living the Gift

U nexpected tragedies, natural disasters, and global catastrophes shake our hearts and our minds. Mass murders, terrorism, bombings, injustice, and chaos worldwide traumatize us daily. Life is truly precious, a wonderful gift from God, but it's also perilous. We never know if manmade casualties or nature's calamities will cut our life short. And the possibility of such devastation exists because there are no longer safe places in our cities, suburbs, farmlands or forests. Destruction lurks everywhere. However, today's dangers must not alarm us; instead, they should motivate us to view life differently and do life differently.

My family and I were in a horrific car accident years ago. Four young men in a stolen vehicle hit us when they sped through a red light during a police chase. Several automobiles collided, ambulances arrived on the scene, and emergency responders quickly aided us. We were injured but alive, thank God. Despite our injuries and this would-be tragedy, we were treated and released from the hospital that evening. The police later told my husband had we been in a different car and had the impact varied by just a few inches, I would not have survived the accident. As it was, I was trapped in the car and emergency responders had to use the Jaws of Life to rescue me. But God, the Giver of Life, was on the scene, protecting me and my family; He denied death and spared our lives. We experienced first-hand the uncertainty of life and the certainty of death.

You can be sure a brush with death produces more than a "thank You, Lord." It produces an alert mind, an open heart and a listening ear. That's why I began seeking His direction while thanking God for His protection. As disconcerting thoughts and reflections troubled my mind, I needed answers after this experience. "Why did it happen, God? What if this and what if that?" were among my questions. A former pastor taught me "Why?" is not the question to ask God in a crisis. Instead, we should ask, "What is it, God? What are You saying? What are You trying to teach me?" Remembering this, I turned my mind, my heart and my ear toward God because I knew there was a lesson in this near-death experience. And you can be sure there was indeed a lesson. God's lesson for me was not about death or our near-death experience; God's lesson for me was about life and living this precious gift called life.

The reality is that life will end one day when God calls us home to be with Him. That's the outcome of our earthly life, and God often shows us life's swiftness. But after our accident, God directed me to the process part, the living part of life, reminding me that each day matters, that He matters, that others matter and that I matter. So, God's response to my "what-are-You-trying-to-teach-me" question was this: Because life is precious, because life is fragile and because each day is a gift, be sure you live life fully, live it right and keep it right. God's response challenged me to be more mindful of my life with Him, my life with others and my life with me. I realize today is my life; this is not a dress rehearsal; it's the life God's gifted me.

As I considered what it means to live life with God, the critical lesson is: I am accountable to God and required to live right before Him. Even though we want to be "large and in charge" of our life, we're not. God holds the deed to your life and mine; we belong to Him. The scripture makes it clear that God has legal rights to our very existence. When God created us, we enjoyed a perfect union with Him. Then we had our way and walked away from God into sin and bondage. We became slaves to sin without hope or help until God redeemed us. In other words, God paid the price for our sins and secured our freedom through Jesus, our Redeemer.

God's unfathomable love and grace orchestrated our redemption. The Psalmist celebrates this with two scriptures, "He has sent redemption to His people;" (Psalm 111:9 NKJV), and "For with the LORD *there* is mercy, And with Him *is* abundant redemption" (Psalm 130:7 NKJV). In the New Testament, the Apostle Paul adds to this, "In whom we have redemption through his blood, the forgiveness of sins" (Col. 1:14 NKJV). Jesus paid the price for us. That's why the deed to your life belongs to God and we should live accordingly.

Because we belong to God, He gives us the ability to live life right and keep it right with Him. No, we're not perfect and we will certainly mess up and make mistakes. But if we make God our priority and right living our purpose, God will help us view life differently and do life differently. After all, keeping life right with God is ultimately our day-to-day, dawn-to-dusk mission. Should a tragedy occur or a disaster strike, we won't have to worry about how we're living.

Think about the profound life principles found in the Sermon on the Mount in Matthew 5-7. After Jesus taught about living right with God and man in this sermon, He summed up its entire message in one verse, Matthew 6:33, "But first *and* most importantly seek (aim at, strive after) His kingdom and His righteousness [His way of doing and being right—the attitude and character of God], and all these things will be given to you also" (AMP).

So, living right with God means seeking God first; it means submitting to God's rulership over us and surrendering everything to Him. "God is in control" must be more than comforting words, a mantra spoken in a crisis. "God is in control" must become our lifestyle where God is indeed in control. As we live like "God is in control" for real, we naturally pursue His righteousness. It happens because He is in control. That's when God has the best place in our life, first place before everyone and everything, first over all we love and all we desire. God in

His rightful place and God from His ruling place promises to give us all things to fully live this gift called life.

And the greatest gift we get from God is our relationship with others. While we value position and possessions, are they more important than our cherished relationships? I'm sure most of us would willingly exchange all of our possessions for those we love. This is certainly the sentiment when we experience the loss of a loved one or the end of a loving relationship. Imagine the heartbreak of people estranged from a family member or friend over minor or even major conflicts. When reconciliation comes, there's regret over missed conversations, missed celebrations, missed memories and missed opportunities. If reconciliation never comes, there's regret over what could have been or what should have been. In either case, God's plan for our relationships is not regret. That's why living a truly fulfilled life demands right relationships with others. For nothing mirrors our relationship with God more perfectly than our relationship with others.

God gave us directions about creating and maintaining healthy, regret-free relationships with one another. And God's foundation for all relationships is love. With this foundation, we can cultivate bonds that edify, enrich and endure. So, before life storms, in life storms and through life storms, our aim is the right relationships with others. Every day we must seek peace and keep peace. Yes, it can be a tough assignment because all loved ones don't want to be at peace with us. Nevertheless, that's our challenge for living life right and keeping relationships right. We have to pursue peace with others in order to secure peace for ourselves.

Living a peace-filled life definitely turns the spotlight on me. You see God's lesson on living life right and keeping life right with Him and others ultimately concludes with living life right with me. What about me? How do I keep things right with me? What does it mean to fully live this life God gifted me? God's lesson came down to this: You have a purpose. Be responsible and fulfill your purpose. Accept God's plan and purpose for you and be accountable to the gift of life.

The lesson is pretty clear and uncomplicated. God has a plan for you and me. He created us with a purpose, but it is our responsibility to fulfill our purpose. He gave us unique and different interests, talents, gifts, abilities and personalities that equip us for our individual purpose and assignments. Yes, God assigned some to minister on national and international platforms, some to serve in local churches, some to work in secular arenas, and some to serve at home and abroad. But He assigned everyone to do what He said to do. Wherever God has placed you, whatever He has assigned you, whoever He has given you, and whenever He directs you, you must fulfill your responsibility in God's way every day. Don't doubt it, dispute it or delay it; you do have assignments to complete. You are not on the planet just for decoration!

When Jesus said in John 4:34, "My meat is to do the will of him that sent me, and to finish his work," He recognized He was here on assignment and Jesus gave priority to fulfilling that responsibility. Now you're thinking, "Yes, that was Jesus; He had the ultimate responsibility to fulfill, but that's not me. I have no earth-shattering responsibility." Too often, we think we're not important and our assignments are so small and insignificant that it won't matter if they're left undone. After all, we don't preach or prophesy, we don't sing or solo, we're not the big shots or the whatnots, and we're not the leaders or the greeters. Granted, your assignments may not seem consequential, not the crusades of Billy Graham, not the songs of Shirley Caesar, not the messages of TD Jakes, not the books of Tim LaHaye, and not the missions of Mother Theresa. But what God purposed for you is your responsibility and must be fulfilled. Whether it's praying, teaching, cleaning, leading, encouraging, sewing, serving, speaking, raking, baking, phoning, coaching, hugging, loving, writing or guiding, you have a purpose. God gave you assignments. They are urgent, God-mandated, God-designed, non-negotiable assignments. They are required; they are not extra-credit assignments.

Perhaps doing your assignment seems trivial or optional to you; and you do plan to obey God at a more convenient time in your life. But let me warn you that dodging the God of assignments is reckless. Such was my post-accident revelation—I remember thinking, "God, I know you've told me to do this, but I haven't, and I know you've called me to do that, but I haven't. What if I had not survived that car accident? I would have left here without fulfilling my responsibility, my purpose. Oh Lord, thank you for another chance. Thank you for an extension on my assignment."

But it's unwise and irresponsible to count on second and third chances. To view life differently and do life differently, we have to be faithful to our responsibility right now; we must walk out our purpose daily. These perilous days and times compel you and me to discharge our duties without depending on a time extension from a gracious and merciful God. God's assignments are central to His plan for your life; they are stepping stones to accomplishing your distinct purpose and destiny. So, when we hear God's voice, we need to jump to it without delay or procrastination. Procrastination will surely sabotage your destination.

How do you view your daily life? Do you value the gift of each moment? Ask yourself, "Do I keep things right with God and others each day? Am I fulfilling my God-given responsibility?" What must you do to keep living God's gift and walking in your purpose?

If you're taking things for granted, taking life for granted, taking time for granted, taking others for granted, taking God for granted and taking yourself for granted, just read today's news sources or watch this evening's news. You'll see life cannot be taken for granted. Life's unexpected events are just that—sudden and often unwelcome. But let's remember this lesson: Life is indeed a gift from God. Since God honors us with life, we must honor Him by living so even the unexpected doesn't disarm us. Live this gift, placing God first and seeking the right relationship with others. Then pursue your purpose with confidence and commitment, knowing God empowers us daily to keep living the gift.

CHAPTER EIGHT

Hope, Expect and Wait

"The LORD is my portion, saith my soul; therefore will I hope in him."

Lamentation 3:24

W'ere living in a time when we all want something from God. I dare say our tears, our prayers, and our cares are focused in the same direction. We're desperate for an end to this pandemic that plagues the world and especially our nation. When you desire something from God, you pray and you hope for it. You hope that God will do what needs to be done, give what needs to be given, and fix what needs to be fixed. So many of us pray daily, sometimes individually and sometimes with prayer partners, prayer circles, church groups, our family and our friends. We're all praying, looking, and hoping for the same outcome—

peace and release from this pandemic. That's our hope, a pandemic-free life.

But I'm learning in this season that our hope should be God and Him alone. Why? Because God is our portion, our reward, and our award. He is your inheritance, your possession, your parcel, and your share. He is what's valuable in life today and any day, in the midst of pain or pleasure. Lamentations 3:24 reminds me that God belongs to us. GOD... BELONGS... TO... US. All too often, I showcase the preceding verse 23, celebrating God's daily mercies and His great faithfulness to me. But even greater than His mercies each morning and His faithfulness is God Himself. Yes, He is our portion and having God is everything.

We have hope because we have God. And we can hope for anything—healing, homes, money, marriage, faith, family, open doors, opportunity, wellness, well-being, things lost, things loved, things damaged, things denied and things yet to come. God is our hope for all. It's that hope that keeps me breathing, that hope that keeps you putting one foot in front of the other, and that hope that keeps us knowing "this too shall pass and the best is yet to come."

God's hope also teaches us that hope alone won't work. We hope, but we must also expect and wait! We have to expand beyond the borders of our hope, from hoping for something to expecting it and then waiting for it. What does expectation or expecting look like for you and me? It means we're actively anticipating something, preparing for it, and taking action before its arrival, even as expectant parents do. They purchase a crib and clothing for the baby, prepare other children for a new sibling, request leave from their jobs, handle necessary paperwork, announce the coming event to others, plan for proper nutrition and rest, and schedule regular doctor visits; their whole life is transformed in expectation of what's coming.

We need to do the same thing to receive what we're expecting from God. Let's open the door or look out the window to see if it's coming. Act like it's on the way. We may not know the estimated time of arrival, but it's coming. So, let's start waiting but not whining. Our hope and expectation in God really require we wait without fear, doubt, and anxiety; we know it's coming, so it's just a matter of time. However, the challenge is learning to actually wait with hope and expectation.

Waiting may suggest to you biding your time or passing the time, but there might be a more active and productive way to wait because just doing nothing as time moves by is pointless. We're waiting on the LORD, so that should remove the spotlight from "waiting" to "the LORD." Isaiah 40:31 says, "But they that wait upon the LORD shall renew their strength; they shall mount up with wings as eagles; they shall run, and not be weary; and they shall walk, and not faint." In that scripture, I like to think of waiting actively, not just waiting to receive from God but waiting as a waiter or waitress before God. We wait on the LORD assigned to Him and only Him. We approach His table, pouring Him our worship as a glass of refreshing cold water. We offer our prayers and praise as a delectable appetizer. We follow with our personal commitment to obey and serve Him daily as the mouth-watering entrée. Then we serve a heart that shows His love to others as the luscious, rich dessert. And when we wait on God in this fashion, He will renew our strength so we will mount up on wings as eagles; we will run andnot be weary, and we will walk and not faint.

We won't faint as we wait on what we're expecting and hoping for because God has His proper place. We won't give up; we won't lose hope or faith. Why? Because we have God. We will live daily in hope and expectation as we wait on God because having God is our hope and He exceeds our expectations. Your life will no longer be an endless series of waiting for life to begin when this happens or when that happens: "When I lose 50 pounds, I'll do this... When I get married, I'll do that... When the kids grow up, then this... When I get a better job, then that... When I move to this place, I can... When I give up this, I will...When this pandemic is over, then... No. Life doesn't begin when circumstances line up exactly the way we want them and life doesn't pause while we're hoping, expecting or waiting on something.

In this scripture, Jeremiah, the weeping prophet, teaches us that God is our life; God is that very thing you're hoping for; everything you can desire is all wrapped up in Him. God is your portion, your fulfillment, your completion, your remedy, and your reward. Part of the process of receiving your hope, your desire, and your dream is to acknowledge that God is. God is your portion, your inheritance; He is what's valuable. When we recognize Who God is and when we recognize all God is, then we'll be in place for God to fulfill our hope, reward our expectation and conclude our wait. God wants to do what needs to be done, give what needs to be given, and fix what needs to be fixed, but first, He wants us to know, acknowledge, learn and understand that He and He alone is our portion.

CHAPTER NINE

This is My "Yes" Season

"Yes, Lord, yes, Lord, from the bottom of my heart to the depths of my soul. Yes, Lord, completely yes; My soul says Yes."

Sandra Crouch

"This is my "yes" season," was my praise report during a Wednesday night Bible Study years ago. Our Overseer was leading a short time of testimony and praise, inviting all present to share words applauding God's abundant blessings. Some people testified to deliverance from drugs, some to victories for their children and some to promotions on the job, but all reflected on God's goodness in their lives. When I stood up, I celebrated the fact that I was finally doing what I knew God wanted me to do for years; I was writing, moving forward on a book He placed on my heart. It was not just casual writing, but I was giving writing my "prime time," the first part of my day when I was most alert and productive. All the tasks that occupied my time would now come after a few hours of writing. I was finally saying "Yes" to God, not only with my words but also with my time, my attention and my actions. I was in my "Yes" Season. Looking back, it was a short-lived "yes" season with an unfinished manuscript.

Fortunately, God has given me another opportunity to say "Yes" to Him and continue working on my writing assignment. Although this current "Yes" season is a blessing fueled by my retirement from full-time teaching, "Yes" has been in my spirit for many years. I grew up in the Church of God in Christ, hearing the saints sing that famous *Yes, LORD* chorus and feeling something special about a "Yes" to God. As I grew to maturity, any gospel song with a "yes" theme reduced me to tears. The lyrics *"Yes, Lord, yes, Lord, from the bottom of my heart to the depths of my soul"* and *"Never say no to Jesus; your answer should always be yes"* both convicted and convinced me of the appropriate response to God. However, most often, I said "yes" to God but did otherwise. Like Paul, I faced the "yes" dilemma he faced in Romans 7: "I decide to do good, but I don't really do it; I decide not to do bad, but then I do it anyway. My decisions, such as they are, don't result in actions" (Romans 7:19 The Message). So while I gave God my "Yes," my "Yes" gave God nothing.

But God has a way of resolving our "yes" dilemma. If we are willing, He helps us transform our "yes" word into a "yes" deed. God wants more than a "yes" song from us, so much more. God wants a "yes" sacrifice, a "yes" surrender, a lifelong "yes" season. "Yes" is a lifestyle for you and me. You cannot fully comprehend the impact of "yes" in your life until you enter and remain in a "yes" season. Just as man's greatest desire in prayer is to always hear God's "yes," God's greatest desire from you and me is to always hear our "yes." That's probably why my earlier "yes" season was short-lived and unproductive. I missed the lessons of the "yes" season. But God is patient, lovingly guiding me to learn that a "yes" season must usher us into a full-blown "yes" way of life.

We best learn this lesson when we understand four aspects of a "Yes" Season: the Meaning of a "Yes" Season, the Importance of a "Yes" Season, the Power of a "Yes" Season and the Reward of a "Yes" Season.

First, the meaning of a "Yes" Season most certainly resides with and is defined by just one word—*Yes*. Although we hear and use the word daily, it seems *yes* presents a problem when it comes to God. We'll respond with a "yes" or a "yes, Lord," but too often, we answer without the true spirit of the word *yes*. A quick look in any dictionary reveals other words used to convey the meaning of *yes*—"agreed, certainly, definitely, exactly, gladly, most assuredly, precisely, willingly, and without fail." But I wonder if your response to God is an enthusiastic "certainly" or "most assuredly." Do you follow His instructions with an "exactly" and "precisely" *yes* or like Moses and David, do you say "yes" but do things precisely as you think they should be done? No doubt your "yes" to God is similar to our brothers and sisters from Genesis to Revelation, a "yes" answer—but with reservation or hesitation. Instead, we need to understand that a "Yes" season is a season in which our "yes" response to God is a clear, convincing and committed "agreed, gladly, precisely, and willingly" *yes*. To whatever God requests or requires, we must answer "yes" and mean "most assuredly and without fail!"

It may be easier to think of a "yes" to God in terms of punctuation. Your "yes" to God must be followed by a period, not a comma, dash or question mark. Too often, our response to God is a hesitant, reflective or tentative "Yes" with a question mark. The question mark suggests that we must hear what He's going to say before we agree to it or take action on it. It implies we have to deliberate, contemplate or evaluate before obeying God. But God doesn't want a question mark "yes" from us; He demands a "yes" response with a period. That period shows trust, confidence and unwavering obedience to God. It's an affirmative willingness to obey no matter the cost or consequence. When He calls, we respond with "Yes," and when He commands, we respond with "Yes" and when He corrects, we respond with "Yes." That's the meaning of a "Yes" season, always a "yes" to God. Period!

We say "Yes," in our daily life when God overrules and overrides everything else. His Word is our standard and His plan is our priority. Jeremiah prophesied, "For I know the plans I have for you," declares the Lord, "plans to prosper you and not to harm you, plans to give you hope and a future" (Jeremiah 29:11 NIV). We, like the prophet, recognize that God's plans are greater plans and supersede our plans. Our agenda goes on the back burner, not God's. We finally surrender our time, our attention, our energy and our actions to God in a "Yes" season, giving Him the main course of our lives andtaking the leftovers for ourselves. It's that necessary shiftfrom a self-serving to a self-surrendering "Yes" to God.

In essence, that shift is the Importance of a "Yes" Season. It reflects a shift in our position toward God, a shift in our obedience to God, and a shift in our standing with God. We are now giving God first place in our life and as we do so, we demonstrate our desire to please Him more than ourselves, even as He desires to please us. So, this season requires humility because we acknowledge that many of our seasons have not been "yes" seasons. And if we're truthful, we'll confess that too often our "yes" was replaced by "not now, not me, not so or oh no!" But in this "Yes" season, we repent, revising and rearranging our spiritual script to a simple "yes, Lord." It's a conscious decision on our part because we've positioned our heart and mind to obey God and obey Him we will.

Therein lies the Power of a "Yes" Season— positioning. There is newfound power when we assume this new position, poised for our "yes" to God. It's a position of anticipation and expectation; we're positioned and ever ready to do the will of God. Picture a runner positioned for a race, hands on the ground, knees bent, face up, leaning forward, listening carefully and waiting eagerly to sprint the moment the gun fires. Such is our position in a "yes" season—hands on the ground in worship, knees bent in prayer, face up to heaven, heart leaning forward, listening carefully and waiting eagerly for God's voice, prepared to move with speed, precision and accuracy.

Given this power in a "yes" season, we push aside fear, anxiety, pride, and even insecurity for it's all about the *yes*. Ears say "yes," eyes say "yes" and heart says "yes." We speak as a zealous, young Mary, "I am the Lord's servant! Let it happen as you have said" (Matthew 1:38 CEV). And we reach our Gethsemane moment when we say like Christ, "not what I will [not what I desire], but as You will and desire" (Matthew 26:39 AMP). Like them, we are appointed and anointed to lay aside everything for the privilege of saying "yes." And make no mistake; saying yes to God is a privilege that has its privileges and rewards. For her obedience, Mary was pronounced blessed among women; and when Jesus said "yes" to the cross, He foresaw "the joy set before Him" (Hebrews 12:2 KJV).

We, too, can experience the Reward of a "Yes" Season. And the rewards are many. For you and me, a "Yes" Season grants a life in order, a life in which God has His rightful place. The weight of disobedience, distractions, excuses, explanations, justification, and procrastination releases us. We're free to please God before ourselves or others. Imagine the joy in that obedience! Imagine rejoicing in the right relationship with God and celebrating our conduct as well as our commitment to Him. God rewards all that. So, as we mark the season with a "yes" voice, "yes" heart, "yes" hands, "yes" ears, and "yes" eyes, we reap the season's harvest; we reap fruit, we reap fulfillment and we reap favor.

The fruit produced in a "yes season" is humility, the humility that comes with spiritual growth and maturity. It takes this humility to say "yes" to God, to surrender to His will and to submit to His authority. It's challenging to humble oneself before another, even before God. But God promises to reward such humility in the "yes" season, giving grace and blessings to those who will. The Apostle Peter makes a good case for showing humility in 1 Peter 5 when he says, "God resists the proud, but gives grace to the humble. Therefore humble yourselves under the mighty hand of God, that He may exalt you in due time," (1 Peter 5: 5b-6 NKJV). What the Greek word for *exalt* means here is "to elevate to dignity, honor and happiness." That promise is our fulfillment in the "yes" season. God rewards us with dignity, honor and happiness when we've humbled ourselves and we're doing what He has called us to do. We're planting, watering, preaching, teaching, singing, and serving but no longer running like Jonah or evading like Moses; we're obeying God. As a result, the fruit we reap in the "yes" season is humility, which brings forth fulfillment.

The final reward of the "yes" season is favor, the favor of God in your life. God has been waiting for your "yes." His word promises countless blessings, but many depend on your action and obedience. Once we're in a "yes" season, we meet all God's requirements, and we're assured of His favor in our life, His "yes" to our request. Remember, the blessing of our "yes" season is in the word *yes*. Most assuredly, your "yes" season with God will produce God's "yes" season with you.

Isn't it time to enter your "Yes" Season? Are your answers to God always "yes?" What kind of "yes" do you give to God? What excuses, explanations and distractions hinder your "Yes" Season? At this moment, let's strive for a courageous and vigorous "yes" to Him, His will and His way. Let's stop putting off what God has called us to do. Too many delays have hampered our obedience. It's time for a firm and unshakeable "yes" to God that says, "Lord, I want to live the rest of my life in a "Yes" Season, obeying You without delay." God will certainly lead us to a "yes" season, bless us through a "yes" season, and keep us in a "yes" season. God's greatest desire for you is your "yes" to Him. "Yes" today, "Yes" tomorrow and "Yes" always.

CHAPTER TEN

Lord of the Harvest

"And the LORD God planted a garden eastward in Eden;
and there he put the man whom he had formed."

Genesis 2:8

O ne of my most treasured memories of my mother is our weekly Bible studies. I remember those Thursday evenings when my mom, my niece and I gathered together around the dining room table, sometimes joined by other family or friends but most often just the three of us. When my mom was still able to cook, a delicious meal frequently preceded the Bible study. The menu included something special we enjoyed, but everything my mom cooked was scrumptious. She never had to coax anyone to eat. I can see her seated at the head of the table with her study

Bible, reading glasses and a notepad. Next to the notepad rested a pen with black ink; it had to be black ink. With everything in place, she was all set and ready to begin our study. I came well-prepared each week, for I had two students eager to delve into God's word.

We explored many topics, but one of our favorite studies was the Names of God. We relished our lessons on El Shaddai, God Almighty, the All-Sufficient One; Jehovah Jireh, The Lord who Provides; Jehovah Nissi, The Lord My Banner; Jehovah Rapha, The Lord Who Heals; Jehovah Shalom, The Lord is Peace; Jehovah Raah, The Lord My Shepherd; Jehovah Tsidkenu, The Lord our Righteousness; and Jehovah Shammah, The Lord is There. We examined the scriptures, envisioned Abraham, Moses, Gideon, David, Jeremiah and Ezekial, and encountered the ever-present, righteous God. In these studies, we embraced God, who is our shepherd, who heals and provides, who fights our battles and gives us peace. Together, we learned how God's names reveal His nature, attributes and character. We loved these powerful studies and the opportunity to share our insights and feelings. It was a beautiful thing, three generations studying God's word. As we studied the Names of God and His almighty deeds, we were like the saints of old who testified, "God will be to you whatever you need Him to be."

Throughout the years, I have learned that God is indeed what we need Him to be. God is everything His names describe; He's all that and so much more. We can experience God in our daily activities. He teaches us important lessons in even the smallest things. He continually reveals Himself to us, displaying yet another name and characteristic of who He is.

I experienced this on one special occasion when I was asked to speak at a Women's breakfast. Since it was the fall season, I selected the harvest theme with the title, Lord of the Harvest, suggested by a dear friend. I was particularly excited and thankful because my mom was going to attend the breakfast to hear me share God's word. While I didn't have a message outlined yet, I was confident the Holy Spirit would guide me to understand our God, the Lord of the Harvest. As I prayed for direction and prepared for ministering, God gave me a very personal and encouraging object lesson on the Lord of the Harvest to present at the breakfast event.

Harvest season is a beautiful time with all that was planted now flourishing. When I think of a harvest, I think of my husband, who loves to grow a vegetable garden each year. He plants a variety of vegetables and herbs, so we usually enjoy a pretty nice harvest with more than enough to share with family and friends. As I've watched my husband happily plan out his garden every year, I've noticed that he focuses on more than just the harvest. The entire gardening process exhilarates him. From cultivating the ground and preparing the soil, to selecting the crop and planting the right seeds, to watering the seeds and pulling out weeds, to sitting in the shade and watching plants grow, to working the ground and awaiting its harvest, all aspects of gardening give him joy long before the harvest.

My thoughts on my husband's gardening led me to the Lord of the Harvest name because it shows another aspect of God's nature and character. You see, in addition to the many familiar names scripture gives God, He is also the Lord of the Harvest because He cultivates a spiritual garden and produces a bountiful harvest for you and me.

Before being Lord of the Harvest, the book of Genesis first identifies God by His name, Elohim, which means God, Judge and Creator. He's our Strong God, responsible for creating everything and giving unusual benefits. Throughout Genesis 1, God lives up to His name Elohim because He makes heaven, earth, light, animals and all of creation. In Genesis 2:4, we learn God's proper name, Jehovah, the self-existent One. From there on, Genesis 2 uses LORD God, Jehovah Elohim, to identify God. It's the LORD God, Jehovah Elohim, who makes man; the self-existent, strong God makes man a living soul. Then Genesis 2:8 unfolds more about the LORD God, creator of mankind. Genesis 2:8 teaches a crucial lesson of who He is and who we are to Him. This scripture explains why I call Jehovah Elohim, the self-existent strong God, the "Lord of the Harvest."

In Genesis 2:8, I see something remarkable; I see God planted a garden. Now isn't it strange that God planted a garden when He created every living thing, the grass, herbs, fruit-yielding trees, etc.? Why plant a garden? If God wanted one, He didn't need to plant it. He only had to speak it into existence.

As I envision this, I see God has created man in His image and now must find the right place for man to reside. When God looked at His entire creation, He found no suitable location for man. Even with all the earth's residential possibilities, God chose to plant a garden as the place for man to live. God did not say, "Let there be a garden." He planted it Himself. Whether figuratively or literally, God planted a garden for man.

Think about it. God could have housed man anywhere on the earth, but He planted a garden for him, earth's first garden. Why? God chose a garden because there's no garden without a harvest and no harvest without a garden. What God planned for man required God's own work, His own tending and care; it required a garden and a harvest. Ultimately, God planted a garden so that man could reap a harvest. And what a harvest God designed for mankind. What a harvest God has for you and me.

Since God planted Earth's first garden for man, what was God's intended harvest? In every growing season, expert gardeners work for an abundant harvest. They protect the plants from insects and severe weather, they provide fertilizer and water for plant growth, gardeners are present to watch over the plants, and experienced gardeners preserve seeds for the next season to promise future harvests. Gardeners do all this to ensure a bountiful harvest. But God, the original Gardener, planned a harvest that far exceeds any we can fathom.

After God created the earth and everything man needed, God planted a garden to give man more. God planted the garden not for man to harvest more from God but for man to harvest more of God. He planted the garden for man to harvest God's pleasure, God's protection, God's provision, God's presence and God's promise. Indeed, God, the Creator, is undeniably Lord of the Harvest.

As God worked in creation, He declared everything He made good, observing it was pleasant, excellent, and valuable. His creation evoked happiness, prosperity, bounty and joy, the perfect reflection of Himself. So once God made man, finding man's idyllic home was God's priority. After looking over the earth's unblemished environment, God selected Eden as the site for the garden, man's first home. Now God's entire creation was good, all prime real estate. The earth was green, lush, and "there went up a mist from the earth, and watered the whole face of the ground," according to Genesis 2:6 KJV. It was all fertile and flawless, yet God chose Eden. Why Eden? *Eden* means pleasure, delight, pleasant and it's no coincidence that God located man's home in Eden. God created man for pleasure and pleasure for man. That assures me that God planted the garden in Eden for man to harvest His pleasure and joy. God intends for us to live in a place of satisfaction and experience His pleasure forever. The Psalmist confirms this when he says, "In thy presence is fulness of joy; at thy right hand, *there* are pleasures for evermore" (Psalm 16:11 KJV).

In addition to God's pleasure, the Lord of the Harvest planted a garden for man to harvest God's protection. You see, the garden God planted in Eden was not a garden like you and I envision. God super-sized the garden in Eden for man's home, planting an 8000 square mile garden, almost the size of Massachusetts. What amazes me more is the garden was enclosed; a fence protected it, surrounding all 8000 square miles. We know it was an enclosed garden because the Hebrew word for garden in Genesis 2:8 is *Gan*; it meansenclosure, an enclosed garden, a place protected by a fence. So, when God planted a garden for man's home, God thought about man's security. He thought about protection.

God knew we needed physical and spiritual protection. Too often, we underestimate the importance of protection in our lives. We don't always need money or possessions, status or position, job success or recognition. Sometimes we just need to harvest protection. Comfort, stability and ease accompany safety and protection. We need protection when we go through difficult situations that make us feel vulnerable, insecure, unstable, unsettled, unsafe and uneasy. We need protection in seasons of illness, loss, family problems and job turmoil. We need protection when going through life's shaking. We need to harvest God's protection daily to feel safe, secure and to breathe easy. I want God to enclose me and protect me. Don't you? I want Jesus to be a fence all around me every day.

Just as God planted a garden for man to live in a place of pleasure and a place of protection, that garden also released God's provision. The scripture says in Genesis 2:9, "And out of the ground made the LORD God to grow..." This verse shows what God provides and in what measure He provides it. God made to grow food-bearing trees in the garden that nourished man and were also "pleasant to the sight;" they were desirable to look at. Here the word *sight* refers to both man's natural eyes as well as spiritual eyes. In addition, when the scripture says, "the LORD God made to grow every tree that is pleasant to the sight, and good for food," the Hebrew word *tsamach*, to grow, means "sprout up abundantly." Thus, when God planted, He intended an abundant harvest of everything that is pleasant to our natural eyes and spiritual eyes, an abundant harvest of all that nourishes us naturally and spiritually. In other words, whatever God provides for us, He provides in abundance. God "abundantly pardons," He gives "life more abundantly," and God does "exceeding abundantly above." God views us through a lens of abundance. When He sees us, He automatically gives us abundant mercy and abundant grace. That's why the Lord of the Harvest planted and we harvest His abundant provision.

Beyond God's pleasure, protection and provision in the garden, God shares His presence there. After He planted the Garden of Eden for man, God visited regularly. God's presence is the greatest housewarming gift to man. As God walked in the garden each day, man harvested the love, joy and peace found only in God's presence. It's not just any peace but supernatural peace, the peace that passes all understanding. It's the peace that His presence gives you and me today. When God's presence enters, the world's chaos exits. God walks in the garden of our life, reminding us He is Jehovah Shalom, our peace in the midst of every storm. His presence assures He's our anchor, our stability and the solid rock on which we stand. He is our hiding place, our shelter, our covering and our secret place. Think about it. God wants to be with you and me. He made the garden a welcoming place to visit and chat and a place to harvest pleasure, protection, provision and His presence. What a spectacular harvest-the presence of God.

In spite of God's presence and the garden's perfection, man sinned and was expelled from the garden. What happened then? Was man's mess-up the end of God's harvest? What about pleasure, protection, provision and God's presence? Was the harvest destroyed? No, not at all. Just as God planted, He also preserved. When man messed up, God covered it up. He orchestrated garden cover-ups for man to reap continual harvests. God sacrificed an animal to cover man's sins in the Garden of Eden, and Jesus surrendered Himself to cover man's sin in the Garden of Gethsemane. Two gardens, two betrayals, and two apparent defeats, yet there remains a harvest. Thanks to the Lord of the Harvest, we still reap what He planted.

We reap because God promised we reap. When the LORD God planted the garden, He planted His promises there, the assurance of His word. God's promise is as certain as His pleasure, protection, provision and presence. Even after sinful man was expelled from the garden and the sin-filled Earth was destroyed by the flood, God still guaranteed harvest seasons. In Genesis 8:22, God made a covenant with Noah that extends to you and me. God promised Noah endless harvests saying, "While the earth remaineth, seedtime and harvest, and cold and heat, and summer and winter, and day and night shall not cease." There will always be a harvest in your life and mine because God promises. He will fulfill every promise in His Word. "For all the promises of God in him are yea, and in him Amen" (2 Corinthians 1:20). Make no mistake; our covenant-making, covenant-keeping God upholds His promise.

No wonder my mother, niece and I loved those lessons on the names of God. We learned as we call Him by each name, God becomes to us what He was to Abraham, Gideon and all who needed Him. And since God planted that Garden, He is our Lord of the Harvest. He will be to you what you need Him to be. He will plant in your life what you need to harvest. If you need God's pleasure, God's protection, God's provision, God's presence, or God's promise, they're all yours. What God planted in the beginning still grows today. Gather from His endless garden. It's harvest time.

CHAPTER ELEVEN

Sufficient for Every Season

"In the good times and in the bad times, in the happy times and in the sad times; having You there made the difference, just having You there (having You there)."

Mississippi Mass Choir

S everal years ago, I faced a difficult season in my life. My husband suddenly became ill and spent time in and out of the hospital. With this illness came a time of fear, anxiety, and uneasiness. I often found myself afraid the phone might ring with news he was in the hospital yet again, and sometimes I lingered on "what if this or what if that." I hated the possibility that our life might change. What I needed and what I craved most during those difficult days was just stability, stability to calm the raging storm, stability that would make life like it was. But when a loved one gets sick, life is never like it was.

Illness is frightening because it hits you with the fury of a tornado, a tornado without any early-warning system. Sickness comes unannounced, unexpected and unwelcomed with an unknown course that can devastate and destroy. Sometimes sickness spins our lives out of control and threatens the daily routine we take for granted. In our case, this season of illness threatened our finances, which was especially troubling since our daughter was heading to college the next year. It also caused me anxiety because I questioned whether God would honor the prayer that I always prayed then and still pray now, "Father, let me and my husband live to grow old together." My prayers battled this anxiety and confronted my fears, doubts, concerns, regrets, disappointments, and frustrations.

Like so many others facing a loved one's illness or their own illness, I found myself navigating an unfamiliar and uncomfortable terrain, a place where it feels like your present and especially your future are in the hands of others. The loss of control and sense of vulnerability numbed me. There were hospital stays, medical tests, and conversations with doctors. I was holding my breath through them all, hoping and praying that the results and reports would be good. There was waiting, waiting and more waiting—yes, the waiting is always brutal. But in the midst of the hospitalizations, the medical procedures and the doctor consultations, I was well-dressed in this calm and tranquil exterior, keeping it "together" for my husband and daughter, holding down "hearth and home" so our lives wouldn't skip a beat. Yes. It was "business as usual" for me on the outside, but I was shocked, shivering and shaking on the inside. I was just "going through the motions" each day. I appreciated all the love, prayers and support from our church, family and friends, but I hated this "sickness" territory and I wanted things fixed and back to normal yesterday. So naturally, I questioned God. "God, what is this? How did we get here? Why are we dealing with this? You know I don't like this place, right? When will You fix this?" "Don't you know...?" I recall asking a lot of questions and feeling a lot of fear, but I don't remember getting many answers because quick answers so rarely come.

Eventually, things settled down as my husband recovered and we resumed the life we knew and loved. It felt good to get back to "normal," so I started to breathe again. Once I started to breathe, I noticed "normal" really wasn't the same familiar "normal." Somehow there was a subtle, underlying change in my "normal." Maybe it wasn't so much an actual change in the everyday routine, but for me, something had changed. Yes, I survived the doubt, the fear, the anxiety and the other paralyzing emotions; I survived them all. When the medical crisis ended, all was well and I was well. Wasn't it? Wasn't I? I'd say more or less, but there was something, something else brewing. My life was back, but my life was different. I felt different. I encountered the season of illness, walked through it with my husband and exited withmore than his restored health. I say more because I felt more, I received more and I became more. Apparently, the medical crisis that challenged me also changed me.

Looking back, I know God worked in me during those months. It wasn't only about sickness and healing; it really wasn't. It was also about me. God used the season of my husband's physical illness to shake and shape me. After months of medical examinations, evaluations, observations and conversations with my husband's physicians, I realized the Great Physician took on my condition. And I didn't even know I had a condition. But God used the doctor's protocol to examine me, evaluate me and enlighten me about my condition. I watched the doctors run tests to figure out what was going on with my husband's health. At times they hospitalized him for further testing and observation. They examined him, reviewed test results and evaluated their findings to determine the illness and best course of treatment. Doctors then met with us to explain the test results, the diagnosis, the prognosis and the recovery plan. We asked and answered questions, shared comments and concerns, and ultimately made therapeutic decisions. I learned first-hand the doctor's standard procedure for moving a patient from illness to wellness. Imagine my surprise that God used the exact procedure on me.

When my husband became ill, God immediately scheduled my spiritual check-up. God examined me, tested my reaction, inspected my heart, observed my thoughts, and critiqued my emotions. How is my health? What's my crisis response? Am I really strong and tough? So how strong and tough am I? God evaluated me, measured my dependence on Him and my disappointment in Him, compared my fear moments to my faith moments, and observed my tendency to resent Him or rest in Him. He recorded every explosive tantrum and each prayerful conversation and weighed my rejection of this season with my acceptance of His season. Who really is in control here? Who is the Sovereign One?

In the midst of a life crisis, God examined and evaluated me to enlighten me, revealing my prognosis and path to better health. Simply stated, I learned God is my recovery and treatment plan. He is large and always in charge. I have a choice at each moment of every day. I can accept His sovereignty or accept His sovereignty. And if those options are unacceptable, I may choose option C, which is to accept His sovereignty. God's fail-proof remedy for me was my submitting to His sovereign position, power and plan, even if it included my husband's illness. It wasn't easy, but I eventually understood options A, B and C were non-negotiable and God was the One in charge of it all.

Given this truth, God gradually changed my view of that challenging season of sickness, fear and instability. He lifted my eyes from the harrowing journey of the health crisis to see His sustaining presence and power through it. He shifted my view, calling to mind He's God and reminding me He and I have a history together. God is trustworthy and I can trust Him. God's word is true and

I can cling to His promises. God is faithful and I can count on His faithfulness through all life's seasons. Yes, even as our family faced the unexpected and unknown, God was there with a healing and recovery plan for my husband and me; He was there. God was present, God was performing and God was perfecting. In the midst of every season, God is present, God is performing and God is perfecting. So in the aftermath of that crisis, I learned. I learned a lesson about life, a lesson about seasons and a lesson about God. God is sufficient for every season.

I love living in Pennsylvania because of its four seasons. I'm sure to complain about the heat, humidity, wind, snow and ice, yet I eagerly await each season's change with the variations it brings. Life, too, has changing seasons with fluctuating weather conditions. Sometimes life is good. We have what we want, life's working for us and we're pleased with it all. Sometimes life hurts; it just hurts. We fail, we lose, and we lack. We're disappointed, challenged and overwhelmed. It's allabout pain and the pain is too much. But that's life, isn't it? Whoever you are, whatever you do, whatever you have and whatever you know, your life is seasonal. Life gives you the best, the worst and everything in between.

Since life's changing landscape affects you and me, why are we rattled when a new season brings a new reality?

From the beginning, God determined that our world and our lives would be marked by changing seasons. "Let there be lights in the expanse of the sky to separate the day from the night, and let them be signs to indicate seasons and days and years," we read in Genesis 1:14 NET. And as God's newly-created world moved through time, He would use seasons to divide that movement, seasons characterized by different time periods and weather conditions, different earth temperatures and environmental features, different daylight and darkness hours and different circumstances and events. Little did I know that God's plan for the natural world would extend to me and invade my space. Then Genesis 8 announces these seasons continue forever, "As long as the earth endures, seedtime and harvest, cold and heat, summer and winter, day and night will never cease" (Genesis 8:22 NIV). That means you and I will also travel through different God-appointed seasons. So tough times didn't begin with me and tough times won't end for you. They come and they go; they go and they come. "There is a time for everything, and a season for every activity under the heavens" (Ecclesiastes 3:1 NIV). Whether kingly wisdom or a noble warning, the Ecclesiastes scripture prepares you and me for life's journey, a journey through many seasons that guarantee change.

While I love the opportunity and excitement of life's journey, I often struggle with the reality of change and instability. Life has weather patterns with sunny days, cloudy days, rainy days, windy days and snowy days. Temperatures range from warm and cozy, cool and comfortable to fiery hot and freezing cold. There are seasons when the daylight outlasts darkness and seasons when darkness outlasts the day. Each season in your life similarly brings change, sometimes desired change, anticipated change, unwanted change and even tragic change. But every change encountered, welcomed or not, alters your condition. You and your life change—your relationships and roles, your physical and emotional well-being, your career and finances, your dreams and desires, your love and your loved ones—something shifts when a new season arrives. That shift, along with the season change, demands we alter our wardrobe, dressing ourselves in clothing appropriate for the season.

Such was my dilemma. I disliked clothing for an ill-husband season; I desired my healthy-husband wardrobe. I, like you, detest seasons of failure and disappointments, seasons of loss and lost loved ones. I know it's often said, "There's purpose in the pain," but can't we propose alternative ways to reach pain's destination? I'd argue there's also purpose in the pleasure so what about that route? Ultimately, however, I learned a season change can be a wake-up call that we are not in control. Yes, we plan but without the power to execute plans, we dream but without the power to fulfill dreams, we love but without the power to preserve love, and we live but without the power to sustain life. The fragility of our life overwhelms us. So what can we count on? When life changes in a moment, in a nano-second, what can we hold on to? When seasons change, "What can we hold on to?" When people change, "What can we hold on to?" When circumstances change, "What can we hold on to?" When we change, "What can we hold on to?" Yes. Seasons change, people change, circumstances change and we change. However, in the midst of all this change remains the mind-boggling message: God remains the same.

Being mindful of our constant God is an amazing, life-giving gift that boosts our spiritual immune system. What a lesson! We're safe in the arms of an unchanging God despite the seasons and changes we face. Because He doesn't change, because He cannot lie and because His Word never fails, I have the stability and security I crave. God surrounds me and you amidst every season life brings. Indeed, God is sufficient for every season and the Psalmist encourages us to believe it with the words from Psalm 31:15, "My times *are* in thy hand" (KJV). Doesn't this mean our times, our seasons, our experiences, our fortunes and our misfortunes are all in God's hands? I believe it does. He allows the season changes and escorts us along life's journey. When God guided me from a comfort to a crisis zone, like it or not, I had to go. Although I followed whining and crying, kicking and screaming all the way, I exited the season understanding, like Daniel, "And he changeth the times and the seasons" (Daniel 2:21 KJV). You see, Daniel acknowledges, as we all must, that God is in control. He changes seasons and most importantly for me, God is present in every season. He has authority in every season, He presides over every season, and He reigns supreme in every season. So yes, I learned God is sufficient for every season.

Yet sometimes, it's really not enough to just "know" God reigns over the changing seasons in our lives. Our mind may grasp that He's God and He's in control. But when a season scalds us, scorches us and shakes our very foundation, suffocates us, paralyzes us, and overwhelms us, our hearts must distinguish who God is right here and right now in this season. We need head knowledge transferred to heart knowledge so we're assured and confident God is right here, right now. Because He is so much more than the creator of seasons and changer of seasons, shouldn't we declare all that He is? God is our Season Companion, our Season Comforter, our Season Confidant, our Season Counselor, and our Season Constant. We should never ever doubt His sufficiency.

God is always present, manifesting His promises at every turn. His presence alone is your lifeline in a difficult season. When He pledges, "I will never leave thee, nor forsake thee" in Hebrews 13:5 (KJV), He vows to uphold you, keep you calm and keep your head above water in every situation. God won't abandon, desert or leave you alone and helpless in life's storms. If the tears flow, your Season Comforter will console and reassure you. Your deep secrets and private thoughts are safe with your Season Confidant. And in uncertain and faltering times, your Season Counselor guarantees, "I will instruct you and teach you in the way you should go; I will counsel you with my loving eye on you" (Psalm 32:8 NIV). That's just the assurance we need because God will not allow any situation to overcome or conquer you, even if you think it will. The moments when you feel most alone and vulnerable, when you feel others have left you or abandoned you, and when you feel hopeless and helpless, God will remind you that He's present to comfort, listen, guide and help. He's there to strengthen, encourage and sustain you.

Through all of life's seasons, God is sufficient. He's not only our help, but He's also our stability. As He directs, protects and nurtures, God is our season constant. We may shiver and shake with changing circumstances and conditions, but learning about God's constancy is our greatest imperative. We must learn who God is in good times, who He is in bad times, who we are in Him, and who we are to Him. Our faithful God, our Season Constant, never changes; He's rock-solid and steady. So when life tosses us and even spins out of control, our constant God is steadfast; He's unshaken in uncertain times.

How I wish we remained unshaken through life's changing seasons and viewed them as life's growing seasons. They are indeed occasions to grow in faith, grace, strength and in spirit. Every season will plant, water, produce and harvest what's needed in your life and mine. Yes. We need to grow and mature, recognizing that a season is temporary, that God is in each season and that with Him, we are Season Survivors.

So even as the seasons in your life change, you too must change. Lean back and let God work; learn to rely on Him and rest in Him for a change. God's message to us is clear and uncomplicated. He is sufficient, no matter how turbulent the times. In fact, the season isn't about the situation, the season is about you and me, our spiritual wellness and well-being. God is greater than any season we're walking through. And we learn this when we journey through a season with God. You can't know there until you go there, and wherever you go, you will find God is there.

I think we all agree seasons are a given. We can expect "in-love" and "out-of-love" seasons, child-filled and childless seasons, "yes" and "no" seasons, youthful-body and aging-body seasons, new-jobs and no-jobs seasons, great-jobs and hate-jobs seasons, loved-ones and lost-ones seasons, true-friend and true-foe seasons, church-work and church-hurt seasons, here's-money and where's-money seasons, new-vision and no-vision seasons, know-God and no-God seasons, good times, bad times, happy times, sad times, hoping, moping, enter, exit, win, lose, and draw seasons! It's life, it's a season and seasons are a given. But so is God. God is a given!

As we enter into new seasons—enlarged, abundant, productive, pleasant and comfortable seasons—we must remember there will also be disruptive seasons. But God is a guarantee in those seasons. He will season every season with His presence and provision, turning our tears into laughter, our confusion into confidence, our fears to hope, our anger into affection, our lack into abundance, our loss to gain, our failure to success, our weakness to strength, our ignorance to understanding, our bitterness to "betterness," and our vulnerability to victory. God is indeed sufficient for every season!

Where are you in this season of your life? Is it a time of joy and abundance, a time of pain and despair, a time of productivity and peace, a time of lack and disappointment, a time of fear and failure or a time of hope and anticipation? Whatever your season holds, God holds you.

How are you walking through this season? Are you convinced God is present? Can you confidently say, "I know God is sufficient for this season?" But if you cannot, and if changing seasons discourage you, challenge you, or frighten you, let me encourage you that God really is sufficient. I believe, like the prophet Isaiah, that God is our stability and "He will be for you what is sure and faithful for your times, with much saving, power, wisdom and learning" (Isaiah 33:6 NLV). We certainly need "sure," "faithful," and "much saving" during difficult times. And that scripture promises us in every season, "God keeps your days stable and secure" (Isaiah 33:6 The Message).

This lesson on God's sufficiency is grounded in God's love for me and you. He wants you to understand that life's changes are a part of His plan for your life. We must pray, "Father, give me the grace to accept season changes and to experience Your presence and Your power in the midst of every season." God promised us abundant life and assurance that He's working all things together for our good. Then we must find peace in knowing He's working, He's working, He's working. He's working in the season and working in you. In every season, God's blessing you. In every season, God's teaching you. In every season, God's growing you. And in every season, God's showing you. Our unchanging God is our Season Companion, our Season Comforter, our Season Confidant, our Season Counselor, and our Season Constant. Only God is our given and He alone is Sufficient for Every Season.

CHAPTER TWELVE

Stay Encouraged

*"It is of the LORD'S mercies that we are not consumed,
because his compassions fail not. They are new every
morning: great is thy faithfulness."*

Lamentations 3:22-23

I should trademark the phrase *Stay encouraged*. It's who I am, what I believe and what I do. If I've prayed for you, taught you, advised you, pushed you, motivated you, comforted you, chastised you or inspired you, it's likely I used those two words, "stay encouraged." I share this message in my many roles as wife, mother, teacher, counselor, colleague, church elder, community leader, family member and friend. It's important to me to stay encouraged because it affects my attitude and demeanor, my walk, my talk and my treatment of others. I remember my mother once said to me, "You wear your feelings on your shirt sleeve." I asked her what she meant and she explained when people look at me, they easily see my feelings, attitude and mood. She was right. I'm not one to hide what's going on inside; my emotions demand immediate attention. That's why it's important for me to *stay* encouraged, not *be* encouraged but *stay* encouraged. These two words are my assignment to the world, whether written, spoken or unspoken. We all must *Stay encouraged*. That's God's plan for you and me.

One of my primary tasks as an English professor is to help students understand the purpose and power of their writing. When they struggle with complex topics and difficult assignments, I ask questions. "What do you want your readers to know and understand? What do you want your readers to think or believe? What do you want your readers to do?" I find my questions help students focus and take control of the task. I want to uncomplicate and demystify the assignment for them. I encourage students, so they realize they have the ability to do the assignment and do it well. As they respond to my questions and encouragement, they often find their voice, their confidence and their direction; soon, they're on their way.

Stay Encouraged

We, too, must stay encouraged because it uncomplicates our assignments and complex situations. Encouragement is critical as we face the challenges that we all have: Health, family, financial, spiritual, emotional, work, educational, social and the list continues. I know my push to "stay encouraged" doesn't fix or change these challenges, but it does change us. It does help you and me refocus and take control of how we view the challenge and how we view our ability to get through it and get through yet encouraged. We must stay encouraged to journey through life whole with our voice and vision intact, still embracing our dreams with direction and confidence.

I tell myself to stay encouraged often. And I ask God to help me stay encouraged when life's complex and I'm overwhelmed. Even in those difficult moments, I recognize the power of encouragement and I want to have hope. I want to be the optimist who sees the "glass half-full" and the believer who's "rejoicing in hope." I want to make lemonade from life's bitter lemons and let "this little light of mine" shine everywhere I go. I want to stay encouraged at all times, but I know discouragement is real and relentless.

Sometimes I'm the source of my own discouragement. The truth is my actions, my mistakes, my decisions, failures and shortcomings may sabotage me, making it hard to stay encouraged when I hijacked my own courage. Maybe it's happened to you too. Then again, perhaps circumstances or the decisions, actions, failures and shortcomings of other people catapult you into a crisis that disheartens, discourages and depresses. But we don't have to remain there, downcast and discouraged. We can re-examine, reflect, release, refocus, repent and return to a place of encouragement. You may see no visible path, but you can find your way back to encouragement.

I learned that years ago when I first encountered Lamentations 3:22-23 in song. "It is of the LORD'S mercies that we are not consumed, because his compassions fail not. They are new every morning: great is thy faithfulness" (Lamentations 3:22-23 KJV). I remember walking into the church, hearing the congregation sing, "Great is Thy Faithfulness, O God my Father. There is no shadow of turning with Thee." With passion and fervor, they repeated the chorus, "Great is Thy faithfulness, Morning by morning new mercies I see." And there I sat, a broken young woman, discouraged and disappointed, unsure of my next step, but I wanted to believe that someone could help me find my way and help me hope again. So as the tears streamed down my face, I sat in the pew and whispered, "God, is it really true? Are You faithful? Are Your mercies new every morning? Can I count on Your unfailing love? Is Your faithfulness great?"

From the moment I asked these questions, God began leading me on the road to encouragement, showing me what He gives and Who He is. Lamentations 3:22-23 is now my favorite scripture and the basis of my *Stay encouraged* counsel. In spite of my failures, God gives me new mercies every day. I've learned my mistakes and messes can never ever outnumber His mercies—His goodness, kindness, favor and blessings. In the midst of today's crisis, today's disappointments, heartbreaks and failures, God gives us new mercies to withstand it all. We don't serve a leftovers God, a God who gives yesterday's mercies, used mercies, hand-me-down mercies or gently-used mercies. Our God gives us brand new mercies, fresh mercies, and unused and sparkling mercies every morning. God has new mercies that apply perfectly to my life and my situation. When I tell folks to "stay encouraged," I'm reminding them that God has new mercies just for them and their life. His new mercies fit us all uniquely. And like manna from heaven, they're new every morning.

God is so faithful in demonstrating His great faithfulness to us. I didn't know the power of God's love or understand how to experience it in my everyday life when I first heard, "Great is Thy Faithfulness." But I do now. When I walked into that church years ago, I'd just completed my Master's degree and like many young people, I had my life planned—education, career, marriage, children and success. But my plan was not working—job interview after unsuccessful job interview failed relationship and shattered heart, disappointment upon disappointment and closed doors in every area of my life. I was discouraged, miserable and saw no evidence of God in my messed-up life. Yes, I grew up in the church but walked away like many of God's wayward children. Now God was pursuing me in my brokenness and the next move was mine. I relented, returned to church, re-dedicated my life to Christ and received this amazing promise of God's mercies and unfailing compassions, "They are new every morning: great is thy faithfulness" (Lamentations 3:23).

I'm pretty sure when God inspired Jeremiah to write those words. God had you and me in mind. Just as God demonstrated His great faithfulness to this weeping prophet, His faithfulness followed young me. The first thing God did was to take me out of my comfort zone. After countless interviews, God opened a job opportunity three hours away from home. Without family, friends, or a church nearby, God became my only support system, the perfect recipe for discovering the power of God's steadfast love and faithfulness. I learned quickly and repeatedly the truth of "great is Thy faithfulness," the guarantee of God's fidelity and reliability. When I searched for an apartment and adjusted to living alone, God provided. When I received an unexpected promotion on my job, God guided me. When I longed for new friends and a place to worship, God directed me. When I faced moments of fear and anxiety, God protected me. During those days, I rested and relied on God's promised mercies and faithfulness. I learned then I could count on Him; faithful is Who God is. Since then, I've journeyed many days with God and I can testify to God's faithfulness in every season, His great faithfulness that enables us to *Stay encouraged.*

God continues to reveal His steadfastness, love and dedication to you and me daily. He knows your season and the circumstances you face right now. If today overwhelms you, God has new mercies awaiting your tomorrow, the next day and the next. God is faithful and always present. When others betray and break promises, discourage and disappoint and leave and let you down, God is faithful; He doesn't change. There's yet hope for you; stay encouraged.

God's plan for you is abundant life and a hope-filled life. Stay encouraged; you know God and have experience with Him. Stay encouraged; you teach others to *stay encouraged*. Stay encouraged; steadfast love covers you. Stay encouraged; abounding faithfulness follows you. Stay encouraged; let *Stay encouraged* become your trademark too. We have reason to stay encouraged thanks to Lamentations 3: 22-23. "It is of the LORD'S mercies that we are not consumed, because his compassions fail not. They are new every morning: great is thy faithfulness." *Stay encouraged.*

Acknowledgments

I began *Lessons 4 A Teacher: Hope and Encouragement 4 You* many years ago when I said, "Yes" to the Lord's instructions to write a book entitled Lessons 4 A Teacher. I started strong and should have finished it back then, not a decade later. But rather than live with regrets, I embrace the encouraging words of my dear sister and long-time friend Verne, who wrote to me at the beginning of this journey. "What God has deposited in you does not have an expiration, nor does this 'season' of writing. You may or may not find that you will not finish all of what you expected before your designated time limit. But who set the time limit, you or God?" I thank LaVerne Mitchell for her wisdom as well as her critique of the book's early drafts. I also want to thank other special people in my life who agreed to review those first chapters and whose comments cheered me on from the start: Pastor Phillip Davis, Katherine Benton, Pastor Betty Burton, Sandra Figueroa Torres, Nickolas Gavin,

Renee' Griffin, Cynthia Matt, Dr. Marcia Theadford, Rev. Dr. Thomas Wright, the late Dr. Glenda Webb and my late mother, Viola Gavin, my loudest cheerleader.

During the seasons when my writing slowed to a crawl, I appreciate those who asked, "How's the book coming?" "Are you still writing?" Even a question can push a writer toward the finish line. And so can a worldwide pandemic. I am grateful for the opportunity to co-author the 2020 book project *Promise: A Global Women's Devotional* with my sister friends Pastor Sharon Scott and Dr Marcia Theadford. In addition, I thank my friend Audrey Harvey for the publishing tidbit that propelled me forward.

I want to acknowledge the publishing team at AMZ Publishing. Your responsiveness, support and professionalism made this process enlightening and enjoyable. Thank you, Frank Shaw, James Dean and the editorial and design teams.

A book about lessons learned would not exist without the family, friends and faith community who are a part of the journey. I thank God for you all. My lessons of faith

Acknowledgments

began with my grandmother, Rose Smith Eleazer, and lessons of love began with my parents, Nickolas and Viola "Betty" Gavin. God blessed me with the best.

My incredible husband and daughter love me, encourage me, believe in me and inspire me. Thank you, Harold and Nicole, for your commitment to me and this book. I appreciate your ongoing review, careful editing, creative design ideas, and thoughtful comments and suggestions. I love you more.

Finally, I thank God for His ways, His thoughts, His timing and His faithfulness. Despite my procrastination in completing this Lessons 4 A Teacher assignment, God is accepting it without penalty and without taking off points for lateness. I'm so grateful. Lord, I'm working on my next writing assignments, and I promise to complete and submit them on time. Thank you.

About the Author

Dr. Sharon Gavin Levy is an ordained elder, educator and author committed to transforming lives in the classroom, church and community. A Professor Emerita of English, Dr. Levy has extensive teaching, training and speaking experience in college, church and secular settings. Her mission is to educate, motivate and inspire others to pursue, persevere, and achieve their dreams.

Sharon and her husband, Harold, are Elders and certified Biblical counselors at Greater Shiloh Church under the leadership of Senior Pastor Phillip Davis and Co-Pastor Kristina Davis. Dr. Levy teaches in the Kingdom Bible Institute and Adult Sunday School, leads a Women's Connect Group and serves on the Women's Council. She appreciates every opportunity to serve others in her church and community and believes "we're blessed to be a blessing."

Sharon and Harold reside in Bethlehem, Pennsylvania. They have one daughter, Nicole, and two beautiful grandchildren.

You can connect with Dr. Sharon Levy at:

Drsharongavinlevy.com

and

Drsharongavinlevy@gmail.com

Made in the USA
Middletown, DE
19 November 2023

42901722R00087